P9-CAA-017

The Early Domestic Architecture
of Connecticut

Published on the Foundation Established

In Memory of Calvin Chapin

of the Class of 1788 Yale College

FRONT ENTRANCE
GRANT HOUSE—EAST WINDSOR

The

Early Domestic Architecture

of Connecticut

By

J. Frederick Kelly, A.I.A.

4880 Lower Valley Road, Atglen, PA 19310 USA

Preface

Timing is everything, and it certainly worked in the favor of architect J. Frederick Kelly (1888-1947). Yale University Press first released *Early Domestic Architecture of Connecticut* in 1924, when many such historical surveys were being published throughout the Colonial States. The new book was well received, selling out its first print run the first year, and undergoing several subsequent printings by Yale through the mid-1930s.

Certainly the timing was excellent for Kelly's practice, as he landed commissions to restore some of Connecticut's great historical jewels, such as the Henry Whitfield House, and to design buildings during the height of the Colonial Revival movement in the United States.

Kelly's book is faithfully reprinted in its entirety here. It is worthy of another round on the shelf, as increasingly rare, fragile, aging copies are still frequently tapped by historians and preservationists who quote his work widely.

Kelly's timing, in terms of both publishing and practicing, was of the moment. His legacy is timeless.

Copyright © 2007 by Schiffer Publishing, Ltd.
Original copyright 1924 by Yale University Press
Library of Congress Control Number: 2006934730

All rights reserved. No part of this work may be reproduced or used in any form or by any means—graphic, electronic, or mechanical, including photocopying or information storage and retrieval systems—without written permission from the publisher.

The scanning, uploading and distribution of this book or any part thereof via the Internet or via any other means without the permission of the publisher is illegal and punishable by law. Please purchase only authorized editions and do not participate in or encourage the electronic piracy of copyrighted materials.

"Schiffer," "Schiffer Publishing Ltd. & Design," and the "Design of pen and ink well" are registered trademarks of Schiffer Publishing Ltd.

ISBN: 978-0-7643-2664-6
Printed in China

Published by Schiffer Publishing Ltd.
4880 Lower Valley Road
Atglen, PA 19310
Phone: (610) 593-1777; Fax: (610) 593-2002
E-mail: Info@schifferbooks.com

For the largest selection of fine reference books on this and related subjects, please visit our web site at
www.schifferbooks.com
We are always looking for people to write books on new and related subjects. If you have an idea for a book please contact us at the above address.

This book may be purchased from the publisher.
Include $3.95 for shipping.
Please try your bookstore first.
You may write for a free catalog.

In Europe, Schiffer books are distributed by
Bushwood Books
6 Marksbury Ave.
Kew Gardens
Surrey TW9 4JF England
Phone: 44 (0) 20 8392-8585; Fax: 44 (0) 20 8392-9876
E-mail: info@bushwoodbooks.co.uk
Free postage in the U.K., Europe; air mail at cost.

The Calvin Chapin Memorial Publication Fund

THE present volume is the second work published by the Yale University Press on the Calvin Chapin Memorial Publication Fund. This Foundation was established November 17, 1916, by a gift to Yale University from Arthur R. Kimball, of the Class of 1877, Yale College, in memory of Calvin Chapin, of the Class of 1788, Yale College, who died March 16, 1851. He was born on July 22, 1763, and at the age of fifteen served for six months as fifer of a militia company in the Revolution. His preparation for College was delayed by the war but was finally completed, and after entering Yale he became one of the best scholars in his Class. Following his graduation he spent two years as a successful teacher in Hartford, Connecticut, and then began the study of theology, though meantime continuing to teach. From 1791 to 1794 he served as a tutor in Yale College, and then accepted a call to Stepney Parish in Wethersfield, now the town of Rocky Hill, Connecticut. From 1805 to 1831 he served as a Trustee of the Missionary Society of Connecticut; took a prominent part in the formation of the Connecticut Bible Society in 1809; and was one of the five organizers of the American Board of Commissioners for Foreign Missions in 1810, holding the office of Recording Secretary of the Board for thirty-two years. In September, 1820, he was elected a member of the Yale Corporation, serving thereon until his resignation in October, 1846.

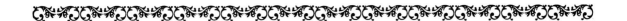

Foreword

IN undertaking this work, the author fully realized that its chief value would depend in a large measure upon the accuracy with which it was done. It has been his sincere endeavor throughout, therefore, to avoid speculation and to make no generalizations which were not backed either by personal observations in existing work or by authentic documentary evidence. All measurements have been made with the utmost care; and where, as in several instances, it has been necessary to depend upon dimensions previously obtained by others from work which no longer exists, the sources of such data have been authoritative.

The early Court Records of the New Haven Colony have been comprehensively searched for all allusions to building and building materials, and such information as the author has considered of interest or value has been included in this work.

Because of the value of comparative dates, a special attempt has been made to assign the authentic date of building to each house alluded to in the text; and in every instance where such a figure has been obtained from descendants of the original builder, or from trustworthy documents, it has been placed after the name of the house, in parentheses. Unfortunately, it has proved impossible to ascertain the exact dates at which many of the early houses were built. In such cases, or where there has existed any doubt as to the accuracy of the date generally given a house, the author has endeavored to assign a *probable* date of building, which is given, in parentheses, preceded by the word *circa*. In a number of instances it has been necessary to arrive at this figure by carefully comparing the house in question with similar ones in the same locality, the dates of which were definitely known.

In comparing the dates of the various houses mentioned in this book, the reader must bear in mind that contemporaneous work in different regions varied surprisingly, owing to conservatism, the strength of local tradition, and the geographical relation of the locality to the principal routes of communication. He must also realize that in very many instances comparatively little of the house fabric, save the framework, is work of the period during which the house was built. Rooms were panelled, ceilings plastered, fireplaces reduced in size, stairs rebuilt, mantels introduced, and entrances changed or added during the years after the original house-building; so that great caution must be used in attributing the date of the house to any of the work within it, with the exception, just stated, of the house frame itself.

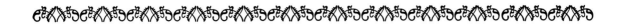

Table of Contents

List of Illustrations

Plates

Figures in Text

List of Illustrations

The Early Domestic Architecture of Connecticut

Chapter I. Introduction

TRUTH is the fundamental principle of architecture. Of the many architectural styles which have, at one time or another, achieved popularity, those memorable few which most creditably bear the test of time are precisely the ones which reflect, faithfully and without distortion, the economic and social conditions out of which they sprang. An architectural style, if it is to be true, vital, and enduring, must clearly and candidly exhibit the spirit of the time in which it flourished—the spirit which is implicit in all the characteristic transactions of the time, and which may almost be defined as the sum of its manners, customs, and mode of living.

The early domestic architecture of the American colonies, judged by this criterion, was unmistakably pure and virile. The most superficial examination of the period is enough to prove that it was productive of a "true" style in architecture. Its building is honest, straightforward, devoid of affectation and sham. The early Colonial houses were true in two respects, both of crucial importance. First, they expressed with entire simplicity and directness the conditions which produced them. Secondly, and hardly less important, their implication was always intensely intimate, *domestic*. They were true to their *milieu;* and they were equally true to their purpose.

The phase of the Colonial period or style which had its inception in Connecticut displayed a number of striking peculiarities, to be presented and analyzed, by text and illustration, in the subsequent chapters of this book. But, speaking broadly and non-technically, the early Connecticut houses shared the fundamental characteristics of contemporaneous work in the other New England colonies. They were extremely simple, and their simplicity was the natural result of a frank and forthright solution of problems which were intrinsically anything but complex. The product of the period, despite its plain utility and simplicity—or rather, perhaps, because of these very qualities,—never missed achieving the fine Colonial dignity—a rugged and vigorous integrity due in large measure to what may almost be called the crudity of the construction.

Consciously or unconsciously, man looks with satisfaction upon that which is substantially and enduringly built. It is primarily, or at least largely, this innate sense of sheer structural value which makes us admire the Pyramids, the temples of Greece, the mighty cathedrals of the thirteenth century. The same instinct infallibly communicates to every observer, even the most casual, the bluff and rugged strength of our old houses; and he who knows these ancient dwellings more intimately, perhaps through having been fortunate enough to live in one of them, is keenly and sensitively responsive to the security, the abundance of strength, which they embody. Their mighty frames of oaken timbers—timbers which measure sixteen and even eighteen inches—have stood unshaken for two centuries or more. By comparison the frame house of to-day, built as it is of 2-by-4 studs which must be sheathed with inch boards to impart to the framework the practicable modicum of rigidity, seems pathetically, not to say ludicrously, frail. He who warms as he ought to the spirit of these old houses must revel in the well-nigh barbaric massiveness of their framing.

It is in this single respect, as much as in any, that the staunch Colonial houses essentialize the epoch which created them. During the perilous and insecure times immediately after the founding of the Connecticut colony, when the colonists, hewing their homes out of the primeval forest, were never free from the menace of wolf, famine, or lurking Indian, there was neither time for anything non-essential nor place for anything flimsy and impermanent. The staunch houses which they built unconsciously expressed these circumstances in every timber of their tremendous frames. Those of their dwellings which, escaping the ravages of neglect, abuse, and intentional destruction, have lasted until now, are a precious heritage. More than any other one thing which we possess, they constitute a momentous and vital link with an epoch to which we owe incalculably much and with a people whose function in our national history nothing can trivialize.

The early Connecticut house is of moment alike to the architect, the antiquarian, and the historian. What I propose to consider here is its specific claim upon the architect and the student of architecture. It goes almost without saying that, to either of these, the natural approach to such a subject is from the historical angle, with reference primarily to the interrelation of various styles, the transition from one architectural period to another.

Granted this point of view, it is impossible for an architect or a competent student of architecture to overlook a certain analogy between early domestic architecture in Connecticut and contemporaneous work of the same general scope in England. This analogy is, in fact, precisely what one would anticipate, reasoning from the historical and social conditions out of which the early work grew. Let us examine in detail, first, the most important of these historical conditions, and then, briefly, one of the more obvious similarities between Colonial domestic architecture and English.

To begin with, Connecticut was settled mainly by colonists of English birth, who, making their way down the Connecticut River Valley or coming by ship from Massachusetts, founded the early settlements of Hartford, Wethersfield, and Windsor. The settlers of the shore towns—New London, Saybrook, Guilford, New Haven, Milford, Stratford—were likewise English. Now, an Englishman betrays few characteristics more accentuated than his conservatism, his innate love of traditional usages. It is but natural that these first settlers should have brought with them, among other things, their building traditions. And even more important, because more fundamental, they brought their traditions and customs of daily living, which would of course exert the most powerful influence on their building. Naturally, such ideas and manners as were brought to these shores did not persist without modification. They were gradually adapted to local exigencies and tempered by the new set of conditions. But, with whatever superficial modifications, the core of the early settlers' life remained English; and so did the fundamentals of their architecture.

Among the colonists were many skilled craftsmen who had served their apprenticeships and received their early training in England. Among the trades mentioned in the early Court Records of the New Haven Colony we find the following: sawyers, carpenters, "joyners," thatchers, brickmakers, plasterers, "ryvers of clapboards, shingles and lathes," "naylers," and "massons." Owing to the system in vogue at the time, nearly every man who did not till the soil or engage in some branch of commerce had a trade, and the artisans of various sorts were highly specialized and skillfully trained, thanks largely to the prevalent custom of serving out long apprenticeships. This fact accounts largely for the skill with which so much of the early work was done, and also for the surprising similarity of the ways in which like conditions were met by groups of men working in different localities. When trained workmen of a conservative stamp are confronted by a given problem, it is quite to be expected that they will solve it and execute their solution in accordance with their early training—that is, in the way to which they are most accustomed. Coming as they did from various parts of England, different groups of craftsmen brought the usages and traditions peculiar to the regions from which they came; only, instead of making a literal application, here in Connecticut, of their traditionary habits of workmanship, they split up or subdivided this body of usage into local mannerisms—a logical outcome of meeting new and untried conditions. But such local types as local exigencies produced were, broadly speaking, very much alike, despite the stamp of localism and the indelible imprint of the builder's individuality.

When we examine the work of these first builders for the more obvious of the proofs that they were indeed working in an English idiom, we find it in the universal and persistent use of a single material for framing. That material, of course, was oak. No architectural usage could be more strongly marked with the finger of tradition. That the colonists, with abundance of other woods, both hard and soft, at their disposal, should have chosen oak, means simply that they elected to use the one material with the working of which they were already most familiar, and the physical properties of which they most perfectly understood. On this basis, it is easy enough to comprehend the almost invariable use of oak, not only for a framing material, but also for exterior covering, floors, and so on. Oak as a framing material continued in popularity for many years; indeed, it can safely be said that it was never outgrown during the Colonial period, and that only after 1800 was it superseded for structural purposes by white pine and other soft woods—and this, mark, despite the difficulty of working, or even handling, so heavy and obdurate a material with the limited tools and appliances available to the early builders. No set of facts could more perfectly express the inherent traditionalism of the English, or serve to show more explicitly the continuity between the domestic architecture of Old England and that of New England.

It remains for us to note in rough outline how English seventeenth-century houses were built. We disregard in this connection, of course, the larger and more pretentious manor houses. The average small English home was a simple structure of stone, "cob," or half-timbered work. A house of half-timbered construction consisted of a combination of exposed oak framework and either "cob" or brick filling between the timbers. "Cob" was a mixture of clay and chopped straw, containing sometimes a percentage of lime. This half-timber style of construction was a very old one in England; the Old English word for build is *timbran*. In Yorkshire, houses of this type were designated as "reared" houses, in distinction from those of stone. During the reign of Henry VIII a statute was enacted which made it a felony to engage in the "secret burnyng of frames of tymber prepared and made by the owners thereof, redy to be sett up, and edified for houses." Judging by the extant English examples of the period now under consideration, a large proportion of the smaller houses were of this type.

It appears, then, that the transplanted English craftsmen—especially those who came from the forested districts of England—on finding themselves confronted with the task of building a house where there was an abundance of oak and clay at hand, would naturally have undertaken the construction of a dwelling with these materials. But houses of this type, though well able to endure the milder climate of England, with its more frequent but gentler rains, which for the most part descend vertically, could not withstand the more violent and driving storms peculiar to our continent. Walls of cob—clay and straw walls—are but ill suited to withstand the assaults of our sort of weather; so that if, as is probable, the colonists did at first attempt this type of construction, they must perforce have promptly abandoned it. But it is of significance that, although a protective covering of wood in the form of oak clapboards took the place of the cob filling of the English panels between the timbers, the structural framework of oak remained as before.

In many other ways, too, the influence of the mother country is to be seen reflected in the early Connecticut houses. Examples are the comparatively low height of story; the close proximity of the first floor to the ground; the steepness of pitch of the early roofs; and the large size of the chimney stack in relation to the general plan—all points to be taken up in detail in succeeding chapters.

In spite, however, of this distinct reflection of English custom, our early houses had decided character and individuality of their own. It would be an egregious blunder to give the impression that the Connecticut house of this period was simply a transplanted or reproduced English house. In reality the two merely possessed certain fundamental characteristics in common. The early Connecticut house, then, was a new creation, wherein the use of materials and the manner of construction were largely the result of Old World tradition, modified to meet an entirely new and different set of conditions.

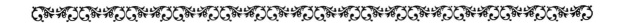

Chapter II. The House Plan and Its Development

IT was the task of the preceding chapter to establish the importance of the part which tradition played in the use of materials and the general mode of construction of the early Connecticut house. It is the purpose of this chapter to consider the influence of the English house plan of the corresponding period, and to trace, from its earliest form, the development of the house plan in Connecticut through various logical stages to its culmination in an ultimate type.

The average small English house of that time was a simple and unpretentious affair of but a few rooms, the first floor of which was close to or level with the ground itself—for in most instances there was no cellar. The use of stoves was rare; and since the open fireplace was depended upon for cooking purposes as well as for heat, the hearth was the center of domestic life. As a matter of course, the chimney stacks were large and massive, in order to accommodate the generous proportions of the fireplaces. To keep the widely projecting eaves of thatch as near the ground as possible, as a form of protection to the walls of cob, the stories were kept low in height. This low ceiling height was ascribable, no doubt, to the kind of intimacy and domestic coziness thus obtained, as well as to the added advantage of greater warmth in cold weather.

We find the influence of these massive chimney stacks reflected in Connecticut. Until a late date the chimneys were of huge proportions, apparently for no direct reason except that of tradition. In considering the various types of house plans, we shall see how important a rôle the chimney stack played in their development. The effect of the low English story is noteworthy as well: the ceiling heights of our earliest houses are invariably low, increasing, however, as time goes on and the old influence becomes less strong. In these, as in more general details, we find specific confirmation of the continuity between the old work of the mother country and the new on American shores.

The first shelters erected by the colonists, we gather from old accounts and traditions, were very primitive and merely temporary. That they should be, was inevitable in the existing conditions: in the midst of an unbroken wilderness, land had to be cleared and cultivated, the attacks of hostile Indians guarded against, and the scarcity of labor and tools offset. All these factors discouraged the erection of anything but the simplest, crudest, and most hasty structures. Lambert, in his *History of the Colony of New Haven*, says: "The first settlements in Connecticut were commenced in 1635, by Massachusetts people. The people from Watertown took up a fine tract of natural meadow . . . which was named Wethersfield, after a town of that name in England. Here a few Watertown men, the year before, erected two or three huts and remained during the winter." At New Haven the first dwellings were but little better than earth cellars, built into the sides of banks and roofed with sods. Eaton and his followers had sailed from Massachusetts in

August, 1637, and there had been no time for the erection of anything better before cold weather.

There is a vestige of tradition to the effect that some of the settlers of Hartford and the towns near by brought with them from Massachusetts the prepared timbers for their homes, ready for erection. There is evidence that in 1633 the Plymouth Colony fitted out a "great new bark," in the hold of which was stowed away the completed frame of a house, with "boards to cover and finish it." The ship was brought to anchor in the Connecticut River and a landing made just below the mouth of the Farmington River, on September 26, 1633. It was at this place that the house was quickly "clapt up."

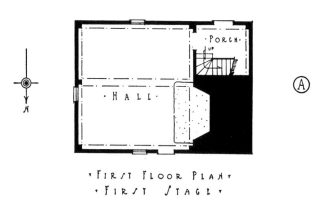

· FIRST FLOOR PLAN ·
· FIRST STAGE ·

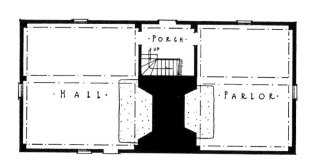

· FIRST FLOOR PLAN ·
· SECOND STAGE ·

S THOS· LEE HOVSE ~ LAST LYME S

FIGURE I.

At first, and before the advent of the framed house, log cabins were evidently not uncommon. Atwater, in writing of the first settlers who came to Connecticut, in his *History of New Haven Colony*, states: "For the winter they usually built huts, as they called them, similar to the modern log-cabins in the forests of the West, though in some instances, if not in most, they were roofed, after the English fashion, with thatch." The Norton house in the town of Guilford (*circa* 1690) is said to have been constructed *after* the erection of a log cabin which stood some hundred feet to the east, and in which the workmen lived while the present house was being built. The Taintor house in Colchester (1703) is the third house to occupy the spot where it now stands, the first one, it is asserted by descendants of the original settler, having been a log cabin. But, as I have stated, these first shelters were only temporary, for the frame house made its appearance early in the history of the Connecticut colony. According to old records, George Fenwick had a "faire house" at Saybrook as early as 1641, which house was "well fortified."

After the brief log-cabin period appeared the first structures which may be truly called houses; and from evidence which exists to-day it is probable that at first they were of one-room plan, a story and a half or two stories in height, with the chimney stack at one end.

NORTON HOUSE—GUILFORD

BEACH HOUSE—MONTOWESE

BRADLEY HOUSE—NORTH HAVEN

SUN TAVERN—FAIRFIELD

PLATE I.

The Thomas Lee house in East Lyme, which was begun in 1664, is, in its first stage, a perfect illustration of this type of plan. From A, Figure 1, it will be seen that the plan of this house was originally that of a single room, facing south, with a great stone chimney at the western end. It is probable that this chimney showed on the outside of the house for its entire height, as it does in the Norton house in Guilford to-day. (Plate I.) The stairs to the second floor were, at this stage, in the southwest corner, in front of the chimney stack. This plan of the Lee house in its first stage may be regarded as typical of the first or one-room period.

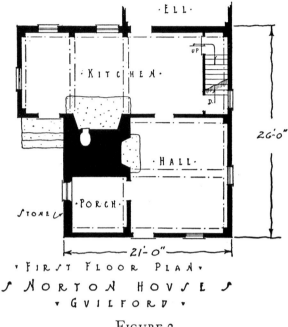

·FIRST FLOOR PLAN·
ſ NORTON HOVſE ſ
▾ GVILFORD ▾

FIGURE 2.

The Norton house in the town of Guilford (*circa* 1690), though essentially a house of one-room plan, indicates, by reason of its lean-to room at the rear, a slightly later development. (Figure 2.) Here, as in the Lee house originally, a tremendous stone chimney, exposed on the exterior, forms the entire west wall of the first story; and although the stairs are not in front of the chimney, there is a space for them there. This house faces south, as did the Lee house originally.

A house of one-room plan, however, was but ill suited to the domestic usages of any except the smallest of families, living in the simplest possible manner; and additional space soon became necessary. It was obtained simply by adding another room, or unit of construc-

tion, on the opposite side of the chimney, which thus became enclosed. This change actually took place in the Lee house about 1690; so that the house then became of two-room plan, with a central chimney, in front of which was the "porch," containing the stairs to the second floor. (See B, Figure 1.) The framing of this second room is quite independent of the original hall, and, when built, was simply butted up against the original structure. It is, in fact, merely that of a single room; whereas that of the hall is the framing of a com-

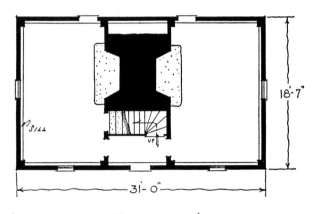

BVſHNELL HOVſE-ſAYBROOK

FIGURE 3.

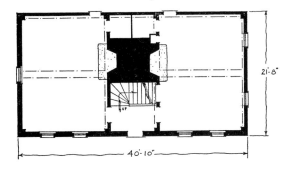

· FIRST FLOOR PLAN ·

♪ OLDER ·WILLIAMS· HOUSE ~ WETHERSFIELD ♪

FIGURE 4.

plete one-room house, inasmuch as it has a space for the stack, which the later room has not.

The house of two-room plan—it soon became established as a type—forms the second stage in the development of the Connecticut house plan. The older Bushnell house near Saybrook (1678-1679) and the older Williams house in Wethersfield (*circa* 1680), Figures 3 and 4, furnish us with typical examples of the period. It will be seen that in each the chimney occupies its central position behind the stair porch. Once arrived at, this arrangement became firmly fixed, and the chimney stack became the center or pivotal point about which the plan revolved in its development. In both the older Bushnell and the older Williams houses a flight of steps leads down to the cellar from the hall. In each it is placed in front of the chimney and beneath the stairs to the second floor. In the Bushnell house the steps are of stone, enclosed on either side by masonry walls. Such an arrangement is always indicative of very early work. In both of these houses the cellar extends beneath only one room. The second-floor plan is, of course, identical with that of the first or ground floor.

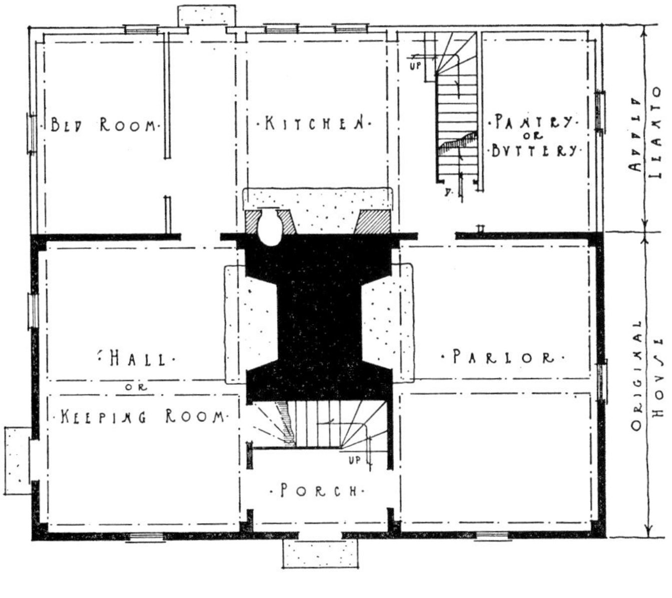

To meet the constantly increasing demand for more room after the two-room plan had become firmly established as a type, the simple expedient of adding a lean-to across the rear of the house was resorted to; which addition resulted in the provision of three additional rooms on the first floor and a large attic on the second. (Figure 5.) This was accomplished by continuing the main house roof in back of the ridge down to the ceiling level of the first floor. (Figure 6.) The rafters of the new lean-to roof were usually a separate set from those of the main house roof, and were framed at their upper ends into the original rear

· TYPICAL FIRST FLOOR PLAN ·

♪ CENTRAL CHIMNEY TYPE ♪

FIGURE 5.

plate of the house. (Figure 7.) The pitch of the lean-to roof was generally the same as that of the old roof above it. When, as in many instances, there is a slight variation in the roof angle, the discrepancy is a clear indication of subsequently added work. (Figure 8.) The lean-to evidently came into use very early in the days of the colony, for the New Haven Court Records for 1649 mention the "leantoe of Robert Parson's house."

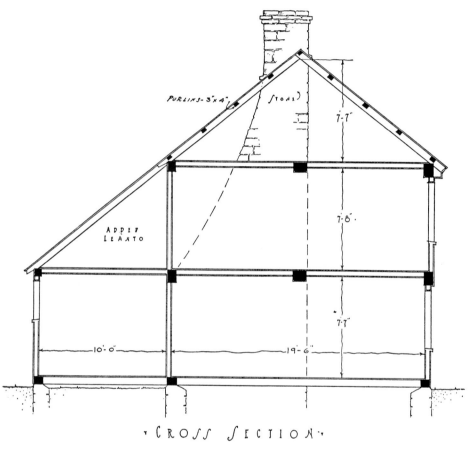

· CROSS SECTION ·

⸭ HARRISON-LINSLEY HOUSE ~ BRANFORD ⸭

FIGURE 6.

Houses of the added lean-to type are of very common occurrence; in fact, this is one of the most typical forms of the early Connecticut house. The Tyler house, near Branford (*circa* 1710), the Acadian house in Guilford (1670), and the Harrison-Linsley house in Branford (1690) all have lean-to additions. (Figures 6 and 8.) Originally each was of the two-room type of plan. An inspection of the lean-to attic in houses of this type generally furnishes the investigator with sufficient architectural evidence to decide conclusively whether or not the lean-to is a later addition or an integral

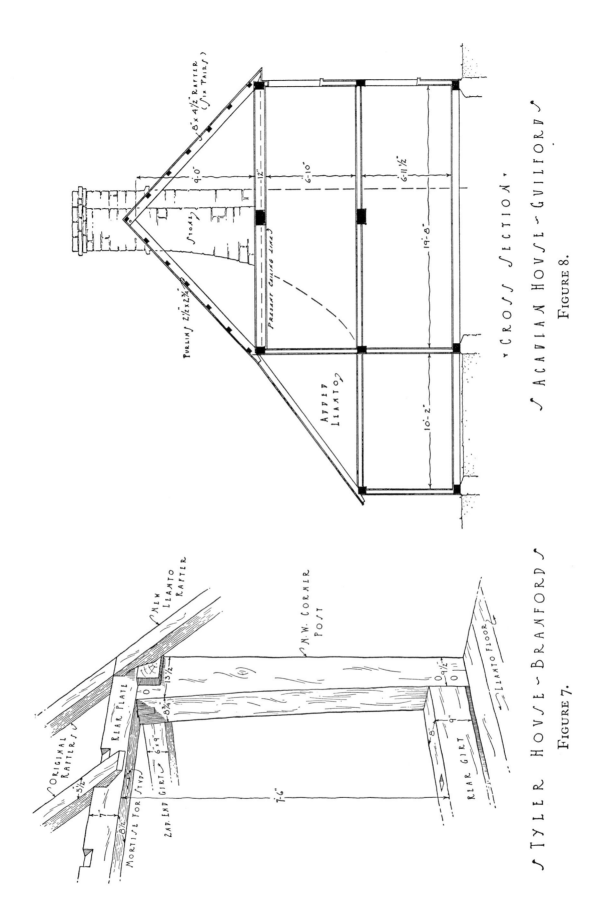

PURLIN 2½"x2¾"

8" x 4½" RAFTER
(SIX PAIRS)

9'-0"

12"

PRESENT CEILING LINE

6'-10"

6'-11½"

JOIST

19'-8"

LEANTO AREA

10'-2"

• CROSS SECTION •

ACADIAN HOUSE ~ GUILFORD

FIGURE 8.

NEW LEANTO RAFTER

ORIGINAL RAFTERS

REAR PLATE

5½"

13½"

8¾"

7"

8½"

MORTISE FOR STUDS

N.W. CORNER POST

6"x 9"

LAP END GIRT

(a)

7'-6"

9½"

11"

9"

8"

REAR GIRT

LEANTO FLOOR

TYLER HOUSE ~ BRANFORD

FIGURE 7.

part of the house itself. The existence of a separate set of roof rafters extending from the rear plate of the main house down to the rear plate of the lean-to does not always necessarily indicate that the rear part is of later date; nor does a difference in level between the floors of the front rooms and of the lean-to attic. The existence of clapboards, however, on the outside of the rear walls of the front rooms, beneath the lean-to roof, is incontrovertible proof that the rear portion of the house is a built-on addition. Old weathered clapboards are still in place on parts of the original rear walls of all three of the just-mentioned houses. In each they are of oak, riven out, and applied directly to the studs. Those in the lean-to attic of the Acadian house still bear traces of the original red paint with which they were covered.

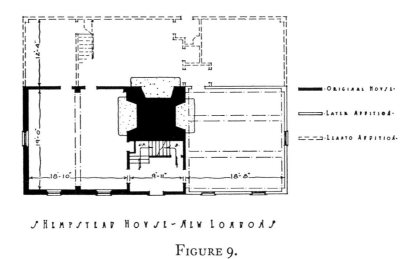

FIGURE 9.

Both the Hempstead house in New London (1643) and the Lee house, which has been discussed, have lean-to additions. From the first-floor plan of the Hempstead house, which is shown in Figure 9, it will be seen that it was, like the Lee house, originally of one-room plan. Later on another room was added on the opposite side of the chimney, which thus became enclosed; and finally a lean-to was built across the entire rear of the house. Therefore this house, as it exists to-day, embodies three different stages in the growth of the house plan. The first-floor plan of the Lee house, as it now stands, is shown in Figure 10. After its plan had arrived at the two-room stage, as shown by B, Figure 1, the house underwent a great change. Up to that time it had faced the south; but, owing to the construction of a new road about a hundred feet to the north, what had formerly been the rear became the front, and a lean-to was built across the south side. This modification of course necessitated a reconstruction of the chimney in the space formerly devoted to the stairs; whereupon the resulting arrangement became what it is to-day. The lean-to of this house, it will be noted, is built across what was originally the front.

The Lee and the Hempstead are two of the most valuable early houses in Connecticut; for each dates back to the seventeenth century, and each embodies architectural evidence sufficient to mark, step by step, the growth of the houses from the one-room plan to their ultimate and present form.

The Graves house in Madison (1675), which is also of the added lean-to type, displays in its first-floor plan (Figure 11) an unusual lack of symmetry, although the layout is typical. Generally the variation in size between the two front rooms is very small, if it exists at all. The period repre-

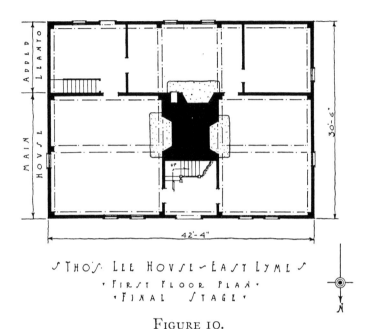

ʃ THOʃ LEE HOVʃE~EAʃT LYME ʃ
· FiRʃT FLOOR PLAN ·
· FiNAL   ʃTAGE ·

FIGURE 10.

ʃ GRAVEʃ HOVʃE~MADIʃON ʃ

FIGURE 11.

sented by such houses as these of the added lean-to type constitutes the third stage in the development which is here being traced.

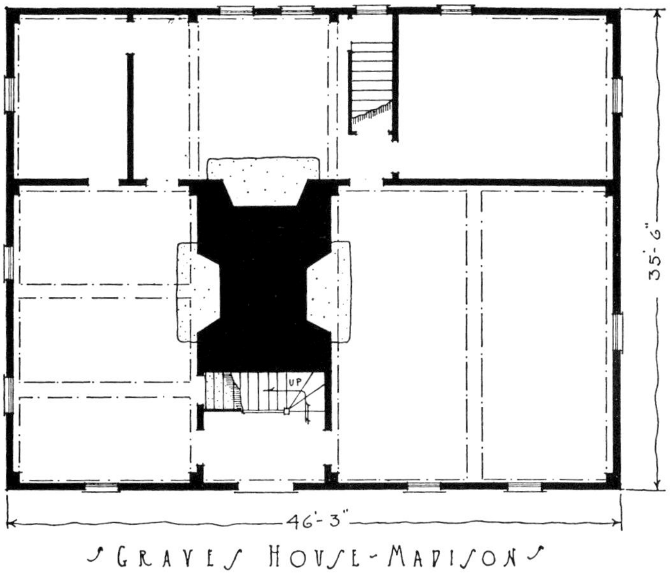

By this period a new generation had begun to take the place of the original settlers; times were rapidly becoming prosperous and general conditions much more secure. There was no longer the urgent necessity to clear land and guard against Indian attacks. Families had increased in size and wealth, and it was becoming possible to devote much more attention to the physical home.

The lean-to, at first merely an addition, presently became an integral part of the construction. The additional space originally gained had become, owing to changes in the mode of living, a sheer necessity. This phase may be regarded as the fourth in the development of the house plan.

The next development, which ushers in the fifth period, was accomplished by building the house of two full stories throughout, letting the first-floor plan remain that of the lean-to house. The most striking external feature of this change is the disappearance

OLDER WILLIAMS HOUSE—WETHERSFIELD

STARR HOUSE—GUILFORD

LYONS HOUSE—GREENWICH

LEE HOUSE—EAST LYME

PLATE II.

of the long lean-to roof, with its fine lines sweeping from the ridge nearly to the ground. (Figure 12.) However, the utilitarian advantage of the change was great: the formerly useless attic-like space of the lean-to on the second floor gave way to three additional rooms of full head-room.

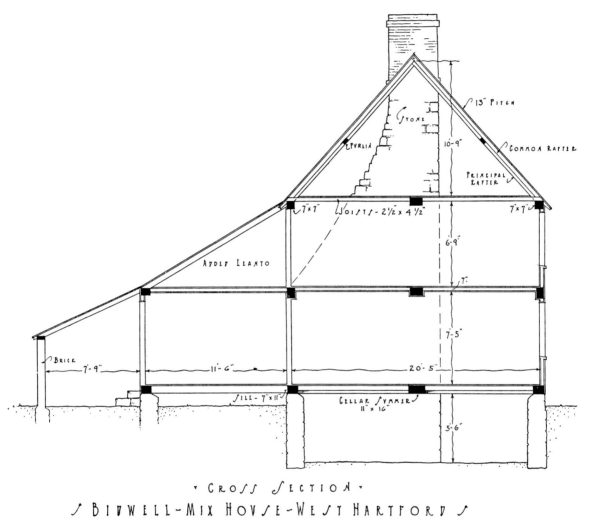

· CROSS SECTION ·
ʃ BIDWELL-MIX HOUSE-WEST HARTFORD ʃ

FIGURE 12.

The plan of the second floor, like that of the first, became a layout of five rooms—the two large front chambers, a "kitchen chamber" behind the chimney and above the kitchen, and smaller rooms on either side of it, corresponding to the buttery and the bedroom of the ground floor. (Figure 15.)

The first-floor plan of the Warham Williams house in Northford (1750), shown in Figure 13, is a typical illustration of the layout of this period. The plan of the second floor repeats that of the first, so that the house is one of ten rooms. On the first floor we find, as in the lean-to type, two large front rooms, one of which is the parlor, the other being variously known as the living room, hall, or keeping room. The kitchen is centrally located, behind the great chimney; on the north side of it are back stairs to the second floor, and a small pantry or buttery, and on the south or warmer side is a bedroom. The sleeping rooms of the second floor were always designated as "chambers," and corresponded in name with the rooms beneath them; as, "hall-chamber," "parlor-chamber." The only sleeping room ever referred to as a "bedroom" was that on the first floor, which was always placed on the side of the house with the warmest exposure. In many instances this room has direct communication with the front room adjoining it.

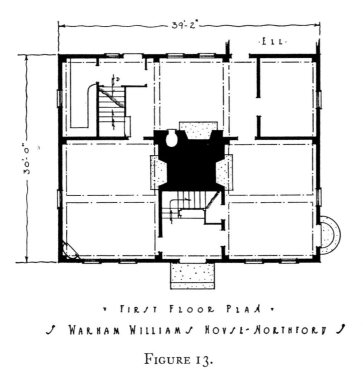

· FIRST FLOOR PLAN ·

✦ WARHAM WILLIAMS HOUSE-NORTHFORD ✦

FIGURE 13.

The Trumbull house in North Haven (1761) embodies this type of plan, as does the Rev. Dr. Huntington house in the town of South Coventry (1763). The first-floor plan of the latter house is shown in Figure 14. Its ell is in reality a separately framed house, for it is of earlier date than the main part and was probably moved to its present location when the main house was built. (Figure 15.)

Up to about the middle of the eighteenth century, when this period drew to its close, utility had been the determining influence upon each stage in the evolution of the house plan. This powerful and hitherto decisive factor now gave way to other influences, itself becoming of secondary consideration. Economy and intimacy of arrangement were superseded by spaciousness and formality; and massiveness of construction was no longer the rule. Rather, massiveness was replaced by elegance and refinement of detail—qualities which reached their culmination at the close of the Adam period.

As may be seen from the accompanying plans, the chimney had hitherto been the central feature, and, from its central position behind the stair porch, had not only dominated, but actually governed the plan. In the plan arrangement there now began a change which must be regarded as of extreme significance. This was the introduction of the central hallway, extending from the front to the rear of the house, with an outside door at either end, and the consequent division of the chimney into two parts. A typical layout of the period is shown in Figure 16. It will be seen that the new arrangement really consisted

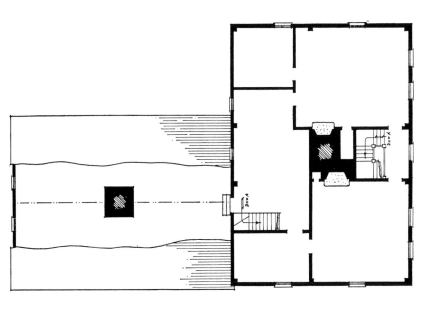

· SECOND FLOOR PLAN ·

↲ REV · DR · HVNTINGTON HOVSE ~ Sᵒ · COVENTRY ↳

FIGURE 15.

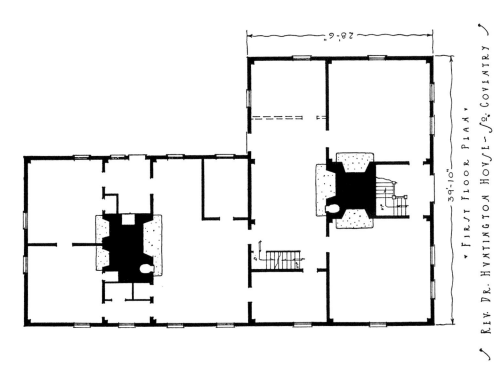

· FIRST FLOOR PLAN ·

↲ REV · DR · HVNTINGTON HOVSE ~ Sᵒ · COVENTRY ↳

FIGURE 14.

of two houses of two-room plan, turned at right angles to their former positions and separated by a hallway which was one-half bay in width.

The plan of the Burnham-Marsh house, Wethersfield (now demolished), which was originally built about 1740, is shown in Figure 17. Its primary interest lies in the fact that it clearly shows an attempt to convert a house of central-chimney type into one of central-hall type. This was done by the addition of a new part at one end, which contained the second chimney. This plan contains the germ which eventually developed into a fixed type.

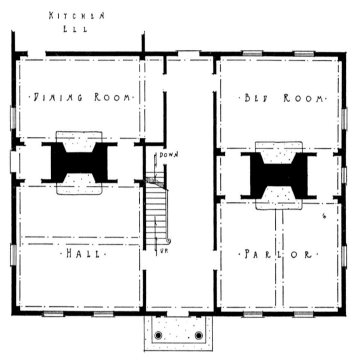

· TYPICAL FIRST FLOOR PLAN ·

♪ CENTRAL HALL TYPE ♪

FIGURE 16.

Generally speaking, the change was simply the product of a search for a more open formation of plan and for a more spacious arrangement. As a result of it, the house plan became more balanced and formal. This balance or formality, so obtained, constitutes the sixth or final stage of the development of the house plan in Connecticut. By the third quarter of the eighteenth century, this new plan arrangement had become fairly well fixed, and it is representative of the majority of the houses built from that time onward.

In certain remote regions, of course, the earlier types persisted until a later time. This persistence can be asserted of any architectural period. Throughout the history of plan development, no precise date can be set for the changes which took place. An overlapping of periods was inevitable, and quite to be expected. The changes produced were gradual ones, and they were influenced very strongly by the varying degrees of conservatism of different localities. Broadly speaking, however, it may be said that the central-chimney plan of two rooms held sway up to about the last quarter of the seventeenth century. During this period the lean-to first made its appearance. From thence onward to 1700 or thereabout the principal changes were the disappearance of the framed overhang, or its reduction to a few inches, and the incorporation of the lean-to, as an integral form of construction, into the house fabric. The period from 1700 to about the middle of the eighteenth century is marked by the raising of the lean-to so that the house becomes one of two full stories throughout.

The central-hall arrangement of plan did not make its appearance until about 1750, between which time and the Revolutionary period, as I have stated, it became fixed as a type.

One important point should be noted in connection with the central-hall house plan: namely, that the first-floor scheme still continues to be the dominating one, determining the arrangement of the floor above it, as is always the fact with the central-chimney house. This dominance of the first floor is probably due in large measure to the fact that the partitions, which were thin and non-bearing, were mainly governed in their positions by the girts or other major units of construction with which they coincided.

It should be noted as well that, as the chimney became secondary to the central hall in importance and the stairs came into greater prominence, the stairs practically did not vary in proportion from those which occupied a place in front of the central chimney. For many years the size of the stairs in relation to the general plan had been fairly well established. Of course, in the general expansion of plan the stairs were eventually increased to more generous proportions; but this evolution did not occur until fairly late.

Many houses of the central-hall or two-chimney plan have a rear ell, a story or a story and a half in height, communicating with one of the rear rooms of the main house. The Pitkin house

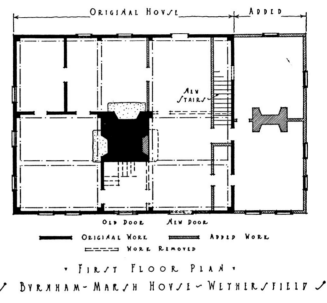

FIGURE 17.

in East Hartford (1740-1750) is an example. (Figure 18.) In some instances such rear ells were later additions, built to accommodate the kitchen and its dependencies, in order that the original kitchen of the house proper might be used as a dining room. It appears, though, both from old family records and from much purely architectural evidence, that the rear ell is very often the older structure, in some cases moved to its position behind the main house, in others standing upon its original foundations and occupied as a dwelling during the construction of the main house. The rear ell of the Webb-Welles house in Wethersfield (1751), for instance, is of considerably earlier date than the main house itself.

The central-hall plan, with minor variations, held sway throughout the Revolutionary period, up to the beginning of the Greek Revival period of 1830. Until that time, it was almost invariably the custom to build the house with its main roof ridge parallel to the

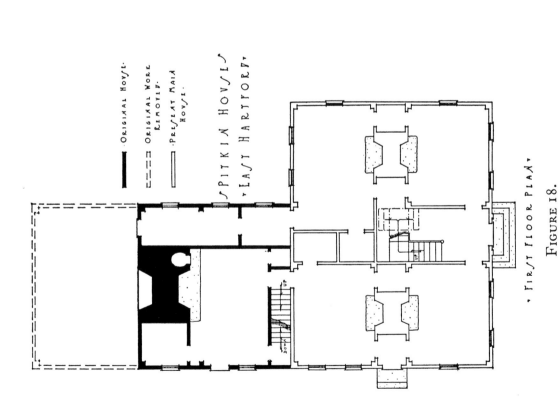

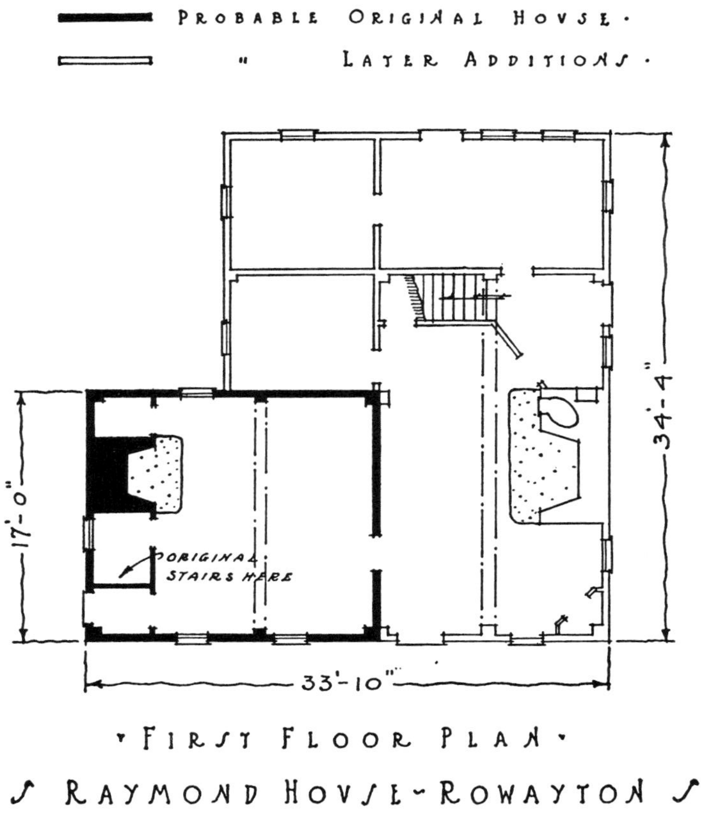

PROBABLE ORIGINAL HOUSE.
"   LATER ADDITIONS.

ORIGINAL STAIRS HERE

· FIRST FLOOR PLAN ·

ᔕ RAYMOND HOUSE ᔕ ᔕ ROWAYTON ᔕ

FIGURE 19.

34'-4"

33'-10"

17'-0"

ORIGINAL HOUSE.
ORIGINAL WORK REMOVED.
· PRESENT MAIN HOUSE ·

ᔕ PITKIN HOUSE ᔕ
· EAST HARTFORD ·

· FIRST FLOOR PLAN ·

FIGURE 18.

street or road. A characteristic of the Greek Revival period seems to be the placing of the house at right angles to its former position, with its gable end fronting on the street. What had formerly been the front now became the side; and this change necessitated a rearrangement of the interior and, consequently, a new plan.

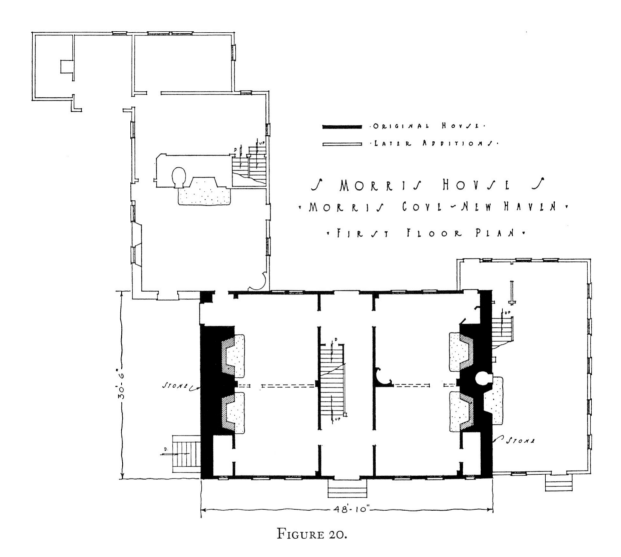

FIGURE 20.

We have now followed the steady growth of the house plan from a simple affair of a single room, through a series of regular developments—each one the logical result of the demands of new conditions, new ways of living—on to an ultimate expression in the comparatively spacious and stately plan of central-hall type; a plan so perfected and so admirably adapted to our needs and usages of to-day that, for the average house of economical layout, it would be difficult to better it.

In addition to the houses of regular plan formation, such as those which have been discussed, and which constitute the great majority, there exist as well occasional houses of eccentric or irregular plan, which do not come under any fixed classification. Of sporadic occurrence, they are exceptions rather than the rule. Frame houses, with masonry ends built entirely of brick or stone, were never common, and but few examples of such construction remain to-day. From the plan of the Morris house at Morris Cove, New Haven, shown in Figure 20, it may be seen that the original house, built in 1670, was constructed with massive stone ends, into which the fireplaces were built. The first-floor plan of the

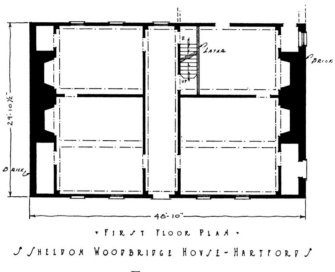

· FIRST FLOOR PLAN ·

ſ ſHELDON WOODBRIDGE HOVſE - HARTFORD ſ

FIGURE 21.

Sheldon Woodbridge house, built 1715, which once stood on Governor Street in Hartford, is shown in Figure 21. The plan arrangement is similar to that of the Morris house, but the masonry ends were constructed of brick. The Timothy Strong house (*circa* 1753), which once stood in Windsor, and which is illustrated in Plate IV, was also a house of this type. The small story-and-a-half house shown in Plate IV, which stands on the Boston Post Road near Madison, also falls under this classification of masonry-ended frame houses. As in the three foregoing examples, the fireplaces are built into the end walls.

Houses of central-hall plan which are built entirely of brick, such as the Chaffee house in Windsor (1776), and the Joel Bradley house in North Haven (1759), usually exhibit end chimneys, the fireplaces occurring, of course, in the end walls. (Plates I and XIII.)

WARHAM WILLIAMS HOUSE—NORTHFORD

PITKIN HOUSE—EAST HARTFORD

TRUMBULL HOUSE—NORTH HAVEN

HARRISON-LINSLEY HOUSE—BRANFORD

PLATE III.

Chapter III. The House Frame and Its Construction

THE framework of our early houses, like the bony structure of the human body, is responsible for the visible form; and therefore it is of vital importance to the student of architectural anatomy, if such a term may be applied to the subject. Aside from its technically architectural aspect, the massive framing of our early houses is a thing to delight anyone possessed of the smallest amount of architectural sense. A feeling of boundless strength, of security and steadfastness, as well as a notable kind of dignity, is inseparable from the ponderous timbers which go to make up these mighty frames. The framework of the early house was a logical and straightforward solution of the problem which confronted the builder; its simplicity and reasonableness are facts simply beyond criticism.

In considering the framing of the early Connecticut house, it is well to take into account the part of England from which the builders in this or that locality of the Colony came; for, as would naturally be expected, we find better and more skillful construction achieved by the natives of regions of the mother country in which timber was plentiful and its traditional use well understood. For instance, the men in Guilford came from Surrey and Kent, the Milford men from Essex and York—all parts of England where timbered houses were common. The Branford men came for the most part from Wethersfield and New Haven; and among the founders of New Haven were many craftsmen and carpenters.

As I have noted, oak was the material chosen by the early builders for the house frame. Distinctly a survival of tradition, its use was almost invariable. Extreme difficulty was involved in shaping and handling it; but when it had once been put in place, it undeniably stayed put. The timbers which we can inspect to-day have for centuries borne faithfully the mighty loads imposed upon them. In certain isolated houses, far even to-day from other human habitations, the tremendous "sticks" which make up the framework excite our wonder as to how they were ever got into place. Certainly, with the limited means at the builders' disposal, their ingenuity as well as their strength must have been sorely tried. The "raising bee" is not so ancient an institution as to be beyond the memory of most of us of the present generation. Doubtless it had its Colonial prototype. The inhabitants of a region must have gathered together when a house was to be "raised," and by their united efforts succeeded in putting together the previously prepared frame.

The main members of construction were of oak, broad-ax hewn from straight tree trunks. White oak appears to have been the variety most commonly used, although red oak occurs occasionally. The framing of the Moore house in Windsor (1664) is partly of hard pine, and the plates and roof system of the Forbes or Barnes house in East Haven (*circa* 1740) are of poplar. Chestnut was sometimes employed for rafters, though never commonly. The use of oak was so all but universal that the discovery of any other wood in a house frame may be regarded as exceptional.

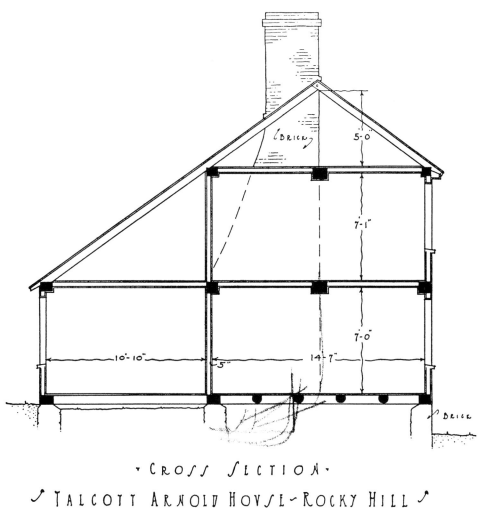

· CROSS SECTION ·
TALCOTT ARNOLD HOUSE - ROCKY HILL

FIGURE 22.

Quite without exception, hewing was the method by which the larger timbers were shaped; it was not until the latter part of the eighteenth or the beginning of the nineteenth century that power sawing supplanted hewing. Even after power sawing was in general use for getting out plank and boards, the use of the broad-ax for shaping the major members of construction was clung to with a curious tenacity. In very late work the framing material was often cut out by means of an "up and down" saw, as the marks on the timbers attest.

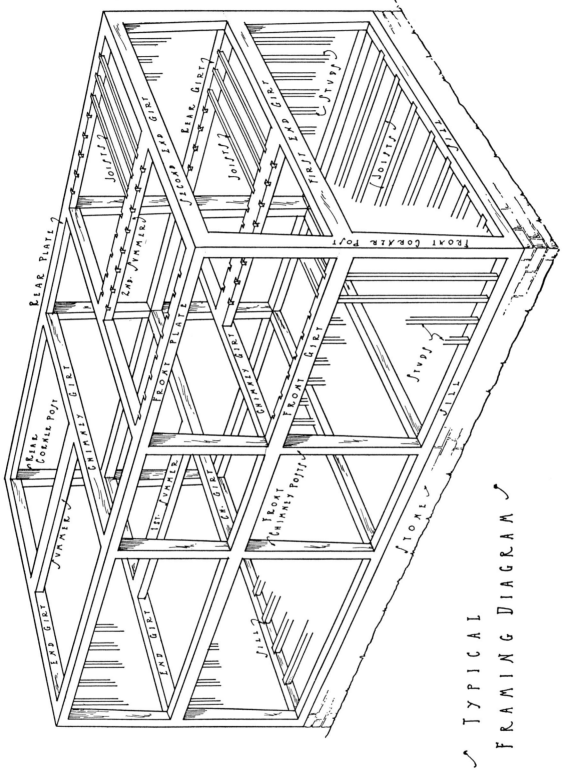

Typical
Framing Diagram

Figure 23.

This instrument was a power saw with a long narrow blade, worked vertically with a reciprocating motion. The circular saw was a later invention.

A general court held at New Haven June 11, 1640, established a scale of charges for both hewing and sawing, as follows: "Price for hewing sills, beames, plates or such like timber, square hewen to build wth, not above a penny a foote running measure. Sawing by the hundred not above 4s.6d. for boards. 5s. for plancks. 5s.6d. for slitworke and to be payd for no more than they cutt full and true measure."

The early craftsmen's skill with the broad-ax must have been very great. In the first houses, much of the framework was left exposed on the inside of the house, and it was given no other finish than that which it received from the ax. Surfaces were produced in this way which were nearly as smooth as if planed; and no doubt the chamfering of exposed beams was done with the same tool. It is obvious that small timbers, such as studs and ceiling joists, could not very readily have been hewn out, owing to the difficulty of holding them securely during the operation. Hence, even in the earliest houses, they were quite generally sawn out.

A typical framing system of a two-room-plan house is illustrated in Figure 23. From this drawing it will be seen that the general scheme of construction was as follows: upon the foundation walls of stone or brick, a continuous horizontal timber, variously known as the sill, "cill," or "grundsell," was laid. The last term may be seen in the General Court Records for New Haven, of December 2, 1656, which read as follows: "The Governor acquainted the Towne that the occasion of this meeting is aboute the meeting house, wch hath been viewed by workmen and finde it verey defective, many of the timbers being very rotten, besides the *groundsells*." Usually about eight or nine inches in its sectional measurements, the sill was bedded upon its broader side, or, in other

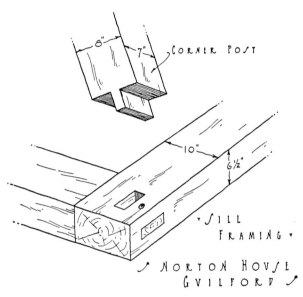

SILL FRAMING

NORTON HOUSE
GUILFORD

FIGURE 24.

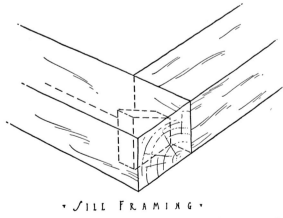

· SILL FRAMING ·

MOULTHROP HOUSE-EAST HAVEN

FIGURE 25.

words, laid flatwise. The corners were generally framed together by means of a mortise-
and-tenon joint, such as that shown in Figure 24. Another and less common form of sill
jointing is that illustrated in Figure 25.

The joists of the first floor spanned the width of each room, and as a rule their ends
were framed into the sills and cellar girts. In a few houses, however, of very early date,
the first-floor joists were built into the foundation walls, and the house sills laid over
them. Lambert states, in his *History of the Colony of New Haven*, that "The ground

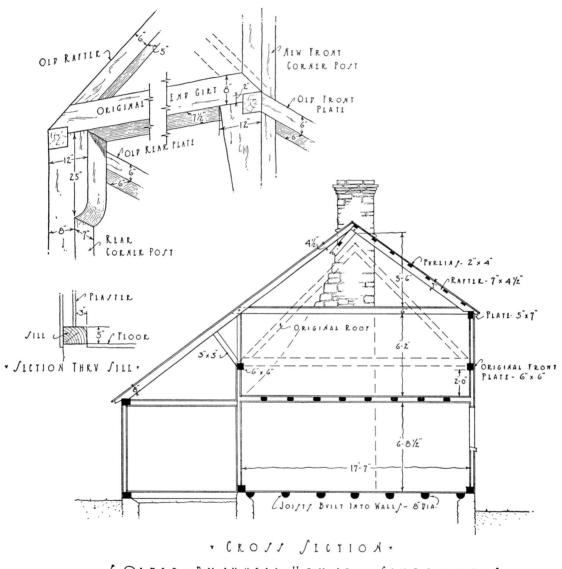

· C R O S S   S E C T I O N ·
J O L D E R   B U S H N E L L   H O U S E ~ S A Y B R O O K J

FIGURE 26.

floor was laid below the sills, which projected into the room eight or ten inches." As a result of such an arrangement, the sills necessarily projected into the rooms of the first floor, as Lambert states, and as may be seen from the cross section of the older Bushnell house in Saybrook (1678-1679), shown in Figure 26. This rare form of construction existed

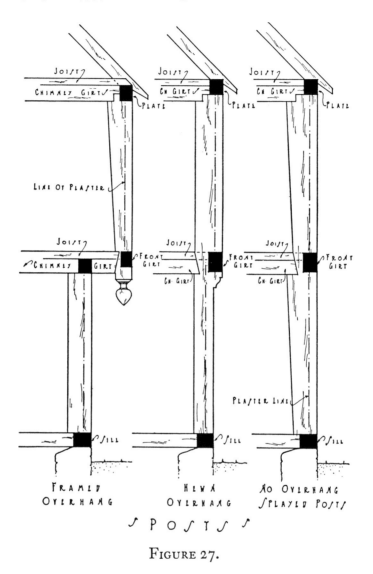

FIGURE 27.

in the Avery house, Groton (1660), and the Baldwin house, Branford (1650), and may still be seen in the Freeman Curtis house, Stratford (1710), and the Hempstead house, New London (1643).

Upon each of the four corners of the framed sills, a vertical member, known as the corner post, was erected. The posts were tenoned into the sills by means of the usual tusk-tenon-and-mortise joint; and often the tenon was secured in place by means of a

House on Post Road—Madison

Strong House—Windsor

Morris House—New Haven

Bradley House—East Haven

Plate IV.

wooden peg driven through it. Where there was no framed overhang of the second story, the posts were of one piece from sill to plate—in other words, through the height of two stories. (Figure 27.) Four similar posts, making a total of eight in all, were also erected—two in the front and two in the rear wall—as intermediate supports. These four posts

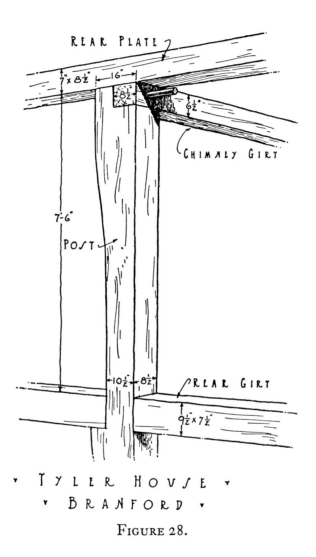

FIGURE 28.

are known as the front and rear chimney posts, according to their position. In the earliest houses, all eight posts "flare" or increase in size in one transverse dimension from floor to ceiling. Accordingly there was a double flare in the total height of each post—one flare for each story. Most often this flare is parallel with the chimney girts, though it occasionally occurs in the other direction—*i.e.*, so as to be parallel with the ridge of the roof. A post turned in the latter direction is shown in Figure 28.

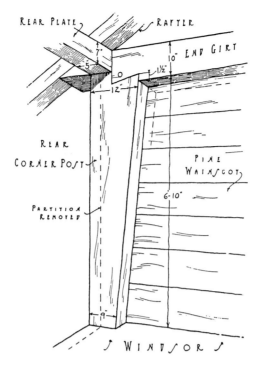

REAR PLATE

RAFTER

7"

5

10" END GIRT

1½"

O

12"

REAR
CORNER POST

PINE
WAINSCOT

6-10"

PARTITION
REMOVED

7"

♪ WINDSOR ♪

FIGURE 29.

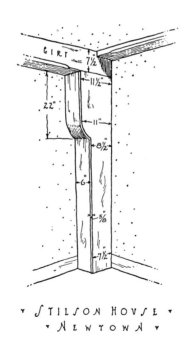

GIRT

7½"

11½"

22"

11"

8½"

6"

5⅝"

7½"

· STILSON HOVSE ·
· NEWTOWN ·

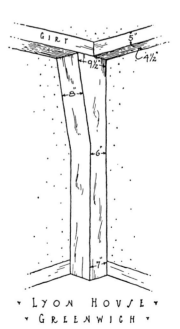

GIRT

5"

9½"

4½"

8"

6"

7"

· LYON HOVSE ·
· GREENWICH ·

FIGURE 30.

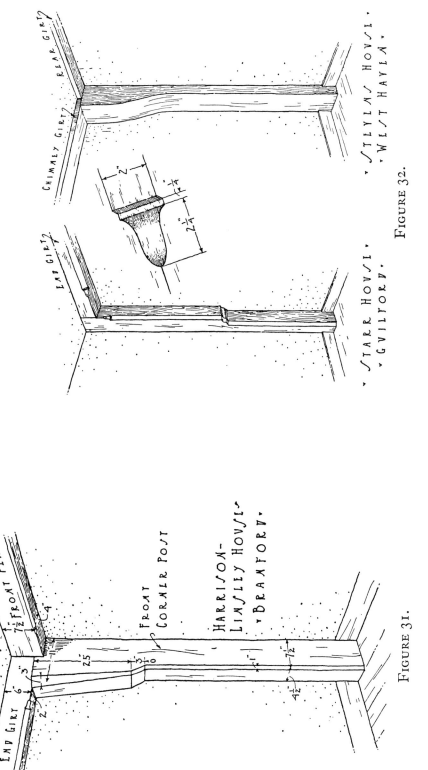

FRONT PLATE

7½"

4

END GIRT

6"

3

2

25

3

0

FRONT
CORNER POST

HARRISON-
LINSLEY HOUSE,
BRANFORD.

1"

7½

4½

FIGURE 31.

CHIMNEY GIRT

REAR GIRT

END GIRT

2"

¼

2¼"

STARR HOUSE,
GUILFORD.

STEVENS HOUSE,
WEST HAVEN.

FIGURE 32.

There are two reasons for the existence of the flare. In the first place, it was a survival of framing tradition; for it is to be found in the half-timber work of England. Secondly, it was done to provide a better seat or bearing for the ends of the horizontal girts which it was the duty of the posts to carry, and which were framed into them. (Figures 29 and 30.) In some regions, principally the shore towns between New Haven and Saybrook, the added depth at the tops of the posts which provided a support for the ends of the girts was secured in other ways than by simply flaring one side of the post. The older Bushnell house in the town of Saybrook (1678-1679) displays posts of shouldered form (Figure 26), a rare device. The corner posts of the Harrison-Linsley house in Branford (1690) project into the rooms, and are splayed only in the upper third of their height. (Figure 31.) Two other schemes are illustrated in Figure 32, that which was used in the Starr house (*circa* 1645) being typical of the whole Guilford school, which was more elaborate than similar work elsewhere. In that region the increase in depth of the posts was very often given a quaintly ornamental treatment. (Figure 33.)

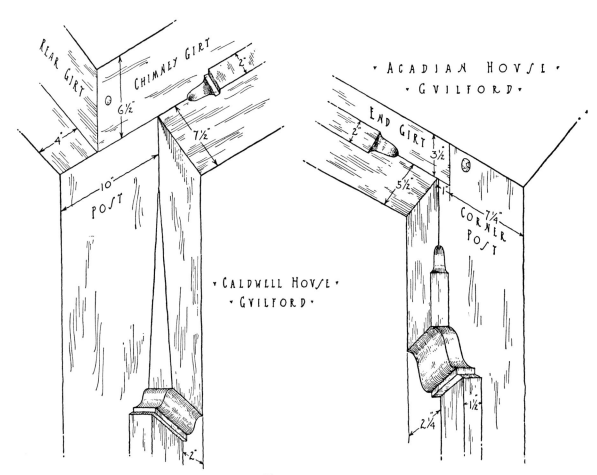

FIGURE 33.

In size the posts were usually 8 by 10 or 10 by 12 inches, although in some houses of extremely heavy framing they were of still greater size. The flare quite generally occurred in the line of the greatest dimension. If a post measured, for example, 8 by 10 inches at the first-floor level, at the height of the ceiling its dimensions would probably be 8 by 12 or 14 inches.

At the level of the second floor, a continuous set of heavy horizontal timbers, known as girts, was framed in between the posts. The girts were of corresponding position with the sills, but of much greater size. They were always greater in depth than in width; if the sectional measurements were 9 by 12 inches, 12 inches would be the vertical dimension. Just as the sills carried the ends of the first floor joists, the girts provided a support for those of the second floor; and the floor joists were framed into them, as into the sills of the first floor, so that the upper surfaces finished flush. The girts are known as the front, end, and rear girts, according to their respective positions.

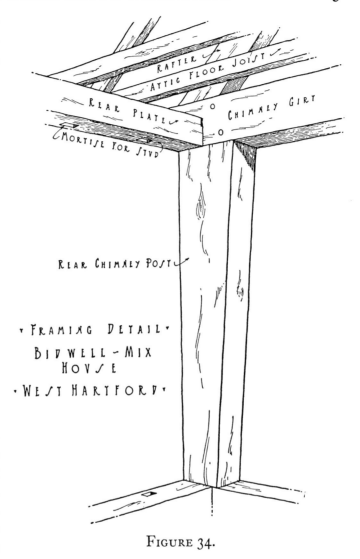

FIGURE 34.

In addition to these girts in the outside walls, two additional timbers, called chimney girts, were framed across the house from front to rear, one on either side of the central chimney. Their ends were secured into the front and rear chimney posts by means of the usual mortise-and-tenon joint. (Figure 34.) It should be noted that the tops of the girts are framed flush, or on the same level with each other, in all cases. The end and chimney girts, because they carry the ends of the summer beams, are always deeper in section than either the front or the rear girts. It is only in extremely rare cases that cambered girts appear, such as the second-story end girts of the Gleason house in Farmington (*circa* 1650-1660). This feature is, of course, purely a survival of half-timber tradition.

From the middle of the end girt to the middle of the chimney girt extended a timber which was generally the heaviest of the whole framework—the summer, also sometimes referred to as the summer-beam or summer-tree. There is some diversity of opinion as to the derivation of its name; it is probable that it came from the Norman-French word "sommier." It has been suggested that it is a corruption of the word "sumpter," meaning a burden bearer (*cf.* the "sumpter mule"). This last would seem a reasonable explanation, for the summer carries a goodly load.

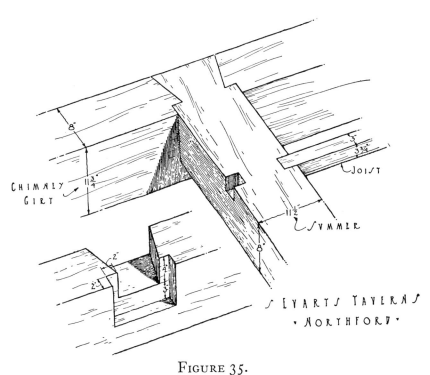

FIGURE 35.

It was the purpose of the summer to provide an intermediate support for the ends of the second-floor joists, which were framed into it on either side, from the front and rear girts. The conventional method of framing the ends of the summer into the girts which carried it was by means of a very ingenious dovetail joint, from which it could not possibly slip or pull out. (Figure 35.) Unlike most of the other framing joints, which were secured by means of heavy oak pins driven through the tenons, the ends of the summer were held in place merely by the weight of the beam itself.

The framing of the attic floor nearly always corresponds to the framing of the second floor, though as I explain in the chapter on roof framing, occasional variations are to be met with. A second summer corresponds to that on the first floor, and end chimney girts repeat those below at the second floor level; but the front and rear girts now become the front and rear plates respectively, and form the supports for the rafter feet.

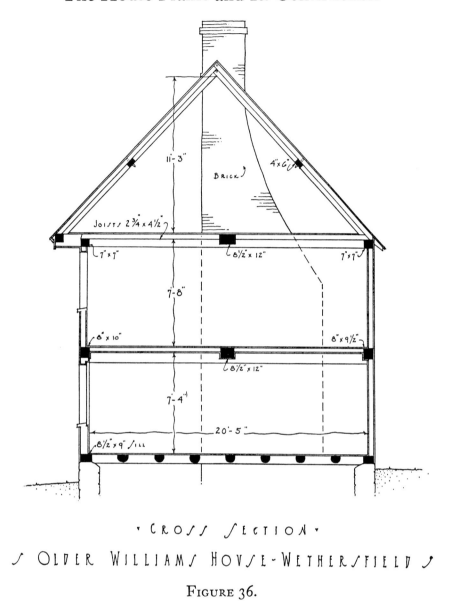

· CROSS SECTION ·

OLDER WILLIAMS HOUSE - WETHERSFIELD

FIGURE 36.

The term "plate" is of old usage, as the following extract from the New Haven Court Record for January 19, 1659, attests: "Mr. Tuttle desired that the takeing down the turret and towre might be forebourne, & that the shores might be renewed, & the plates lined where they were weake." The building referred to is the old meeting house which at that time stood upon the Green.

The rear plate was usually framed in the conventional way, in line with the girt below it; but a great deal of variation is to be met with in the placing of the front plate. Whatever arrangement was resorted to by the builders, their object was the same in every case: namely, to project the outer face of the plate beyond the house line sufficiently to

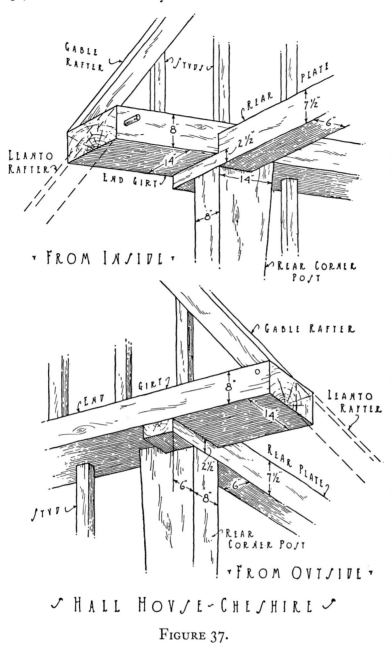

GABLE RAFTER

STUDS

PLATE

REAR

7½"

8

2½

6"

LEANTO RAFTERS

14

END GIRT

14

8

FROM INSIDE

REAR CORNER POST

GABLE RAFTER

END GIRT

8

LEANTO RAFTER

14

2½

STUD

6

8

6

7½"

REAR PLATE

STUDS

REAR CORNER POST

FROM OUTSIDE

HALL HOUSE-CHESHIRE

FIGURE 37.

serve as a foundation for cornice construction. Much and varied ingenuity is to be seen in the various framing methods which were put into play. Perhaps the commonest practice was to frame a second plate out beyond the first plate, which was on the house line. From Figure 36, a typical example, it will be seen that the second plate is supported by the projecting ends of the second-floor girts, which are halved over the first plate where they cross it. Other forms of front plate framing are treated in detail in Chapter XII, The Main Cornice.

Some variation is to be met with in the manner of framing the second end girts, which form the base of the gable. The projecting or overhanging gable was a common feature of early work, and it persisted in modified form until a late date. Where the gable does overhang, its projection is secured in one of two ways: either by framing out the end girt beyond the house line, by means of the supporting ends of the plates which were extended for that purpose; or by framing a second end girt outside the first one, which was in its usual position. The latter arrangement, which exists in the Stowe house, Milford (1685-1690), and the Moore house, Windsor (1664), is comparatively rare. A typical instance of gable overhang secured by framing out the end girt is to be seen in the Hall house, Cheshire (1730). Its construction is shown in detail in Figure 37. (Also see Plate XVII.)

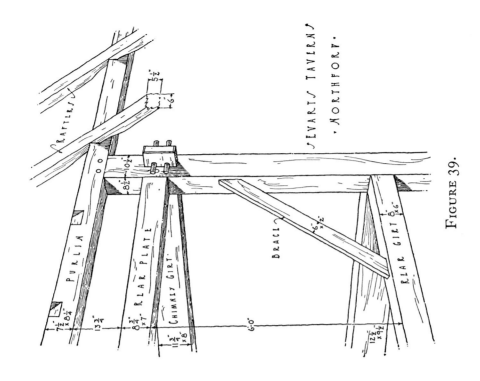

FIGURE 39.

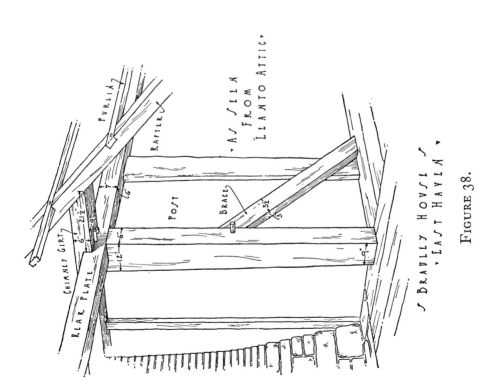

FIGURE 38.

Braces, when used, were commonly framed in diagonally between posts and first-floor girts; though very often the order was reversed, and the braces ran from the posts up to the plates and second end girts. (Figures 38 and 39.) Many houses display a complete system of bracing, which commonly occurs in outside walls.

To return to the sills: we find that the first-floor joists were in every case framed into them in such a manner that the tops of the sills and the tops of the joists finished flush, as I have stated. In most cases, the first-floor joists were simply rough logs, from six to ten inches in diameter, with the upper surfaces hewn off so as to provide a flat surface to which

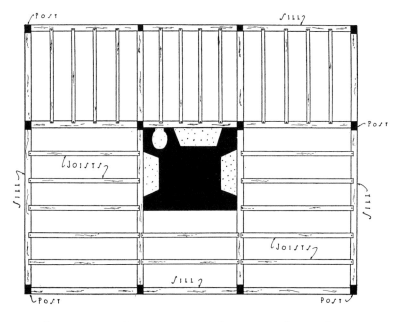

↗ Typical First Floor Framing Plan ↙

FIGURE 40.

the floor boards could be nailed. As they were exposed only in the cellar, the bark was usually left on these joists, which were spaced from two to three feet on centers. In direction, the first-floor joists extended in almost every case from the end sills to the cellar chimney girts, so that they ran parallel with the front of the house. A typical first-floor framing plan is given in Figure 40. Occasionally a variation of this system is found, in which a cellar summer occurs. The joists are then framed into this beam, and run to it from the front and rear sills. Such an arrangement may be seen in the cross section of the Bidwell-Mix house in West Hartford (1695-1700), shown in Figure 12. The cellar summer in this instance measures 11 by 16 inches in section, and is broad-ax hewn on all four sides. A cellar summer may also be seen in the Stevens house, West Haven (1735), although in this case it extends from the front to the rear sill, and the first-floor joists are framed into

General Walker House—Stratford

Wildman House—Brookfield

Stone House—Guilford

Pardee House—Montowese

Plate V.

it from the cellar chimney girt and the end sill, on either side. This timber, which is also hewn, measures 8½ inches in depth by 11 inches in width.

A typical framing plan of the second floor of a house of lean-to type is shown in Figure 41, from which it will be seen that it very closely approximated that of the first or ground floor; the principal difference being in the decreased size of the floor joists, due to the presence of the summers. In the earliest houses, before the advent of plastering, the second- and attic-floor joists were left exposed, appearing against the ceilings or the under sides of the floors above them. Such joists were always of comparatively small size; sectional measurements of those in the Caleb Dudley house in North Guilford (*circa* 1690) show

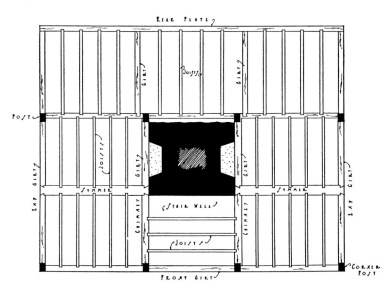

TYPICAL SECOND FLOOR FRAMING PLAN

FIGURE 41.

them to be 2¾ by 3½ inches, of those in the Nathaniel Strong house in Windsor (1698), 2½ by 4½ inches, and of those in the Deacon Stephen Hotchkiss house in Cheshire (*circa* 1730), 3 by 3½ inches.

As I have already noted, these joists, because of the difficulty of hewing timbers so small, were sawn or split from logs or larger timbers. When left exposed, they were carefully planed, and the lower corners either slightly chamfered or finished with a three-quarter bead, measuring from ⅜ to ½ inch. The second-floor joists were always framed into their supporting beams so that the tops of all finished flush; whereas the attic-floor joists, in some houses, were placed upon the plates, and not framed into them. (Figure 34.) This arrangement also exists in the older Williams house in Wethersfield (*circa* 1680). (Figure 126.) Construction of this sort, a characteristic of very early work, is comparatively rare. The average spacing of both second- and attic-floor joists was in the neigh-

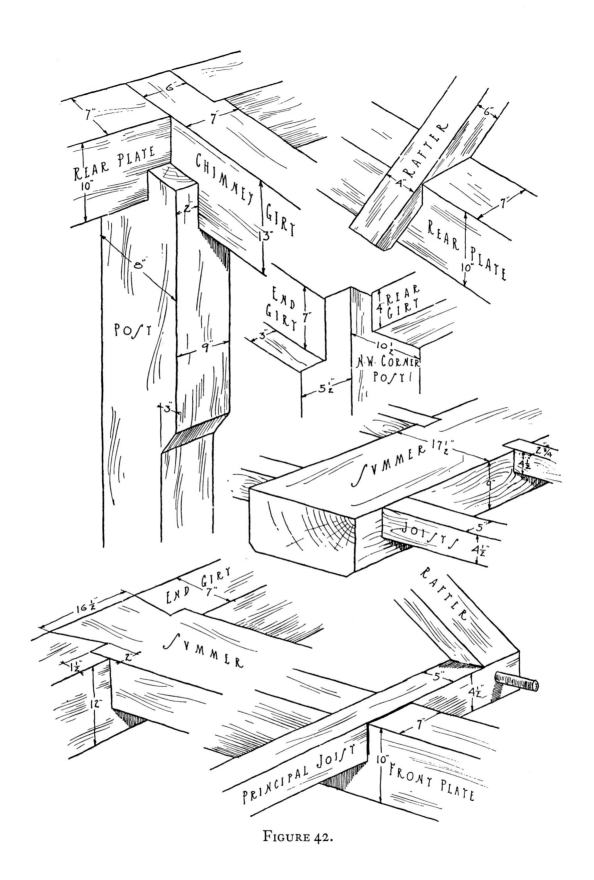

FIGURE 42.

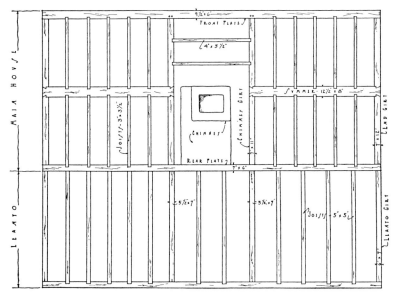

· ATTIC FRAMING PLAN ·
· MOULTHROP HOUSE - EAST HAVEN ·

FIGURE 43.

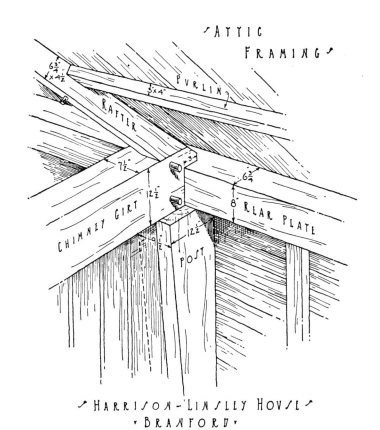

· ATTIC FRAMING ·

· HARRISON - LINSLEY HOUSE ·
· BRANFORD ·

FIGURE 44.

borhood of twenty inches on centers. A framing plan of the Moulthrop house (*circa* 1690), which formerly stood in East Haven, is shown in Figure 43. It is typical of the central-chimney house of lean-to type.

The studs, or intermediate framing members of the exterior walls, were also small timbers, generally measuring about 2½ by 3 inches in section. In height they were only the distance between two horizontal members of construction; for instance, one set of studs ran from the sill to the first girt, and the second set from the first girt to the plate. Inasmuch as the studs bore no vertical load, they were naturally small; still, their ends

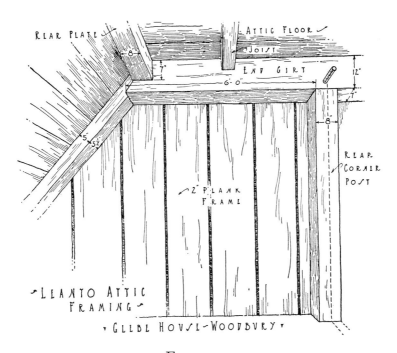

FIGURE 45.

were always framed into the beams at the top and bottom by means of the usual tusk-tenon-and-mortise joint. The outside faces of the studs, and the main members of construction which held them, were in all cases framed flush. Like the joists, they were almost always sawed, rather than hewn. They were spaced from twenty inches to two feet on centers.

The studs of the interior walls or partitions were similar in size and spacing. Very often, 1¼- or 1½-inch oak planks were used in their stead, as a foundation to which the lath could be nailed.

In Connecticut there exist a large number of so-called "plank-frame" houses, in the construction of which oak planks of from 1¼ to 2 inches in thickness were used in the outside walls, in place of the usual studs. In such houses, of which the Norton house in the town of Guilford (*circa* 1690) is a typical example, the planks were applied vertically, and extended in one unbroken length from sill to plate. Varying in width from 12 to 15 inches, or even more, they were secured to the main framework, which was the same as that of a studded house, by means of oak pins about three-quarters of an inch in diameter. These pins were driven through holes bored through the planks and into the sills, girts, and plates. Usually two pins were placed at each bearing. The planking of the Norton house is placed

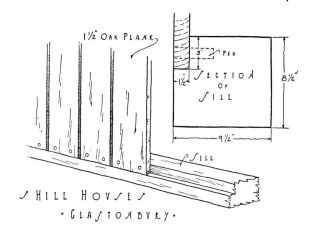

FIGURE 46.

so that spaces of about two inches' width occur between the planks. These spaces were plugged with a mixture of clay and cut straw. In some cases, as Figure 46 shows, the planks were set into a rabbet cut in the sill.

There is, on the whole, very little variation from the framing scheme just described. Minor differences occasionally occur, but the major members of construction do not vary. During the period of the lean-to, the end sills were extended and a new rear sill was placed

upon the new foundations; two new corner posts, one story high, were erected, as well as two new rear chimney posts, so that the total number became twelve, instead of eight, as formerly. Upon these four new rear posts was placed the new rear plate of the lean-to, at the level of the old rear girt, as illustrated in Figure 8. New end girts were framed in between the old and the new rear corner posts, and, parallel with them, extensions of the chimney girts back to the new rear chimney posts. Figure 47 shows the method whereby the extensions of the chimney girts were sometimes framed into the old rear girts. The ceiling joists of the lean-to ran from the old rear girts to the new rear lean-to plate. (Figure 6.) When the lean-to became an organic part of the house, this framing became integral with that of the main body of the house. In this event the old rear girt becomes in reality a second summer, though, unlike the first one, it does not appear across the ceiling of a room.

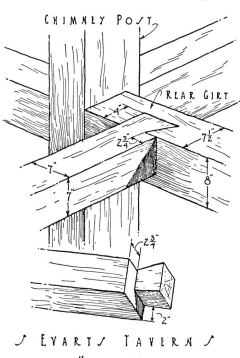

EVARTS TAVERN
NORTHFORD

FIGURE 47.

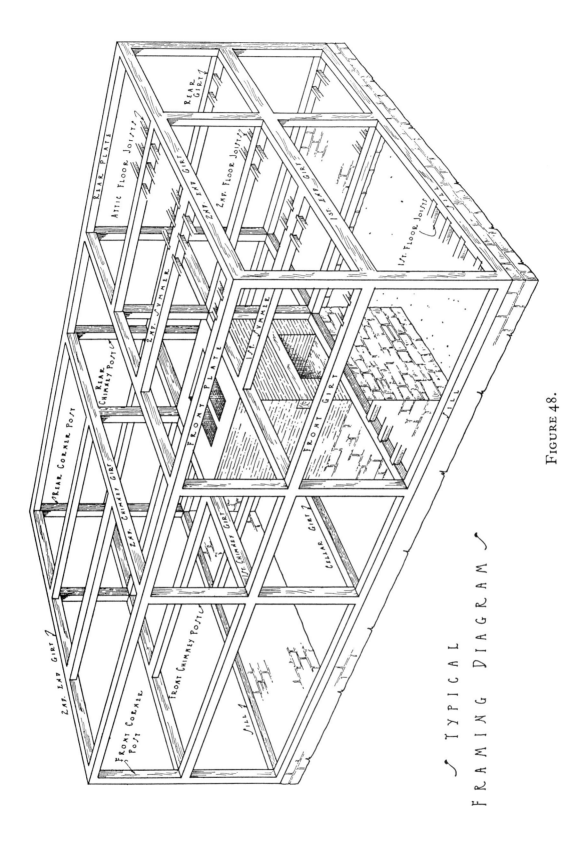

REAR PLATE

REAR GIRT

ATTIC FLOOR JOISTS

2ND. END GIRT

2ND. FLOOR JOISTS

1ST. END GIRT

1ST. FLOOR JOISTS

SILL

2ND. SUMMER

1ST. SUMMER

FRONT PLATE

FRONT GIRT

REAR CHIMNEY POST

REAR CORNER POST

2ND. CHIMNEY GIRT

2ND. END GIRT

1ST. CHIMNEY GIRT

CELLAR GIRT

FRONT CHIMNEY POST

FRONT CORNER POST

SILL

SILL

~ TYPICAL ~
FRAMING DIAGRAM

FIGURE 48.

During the next step, when the lean-to disappears and the house becomes of two full stories throughout, the full number of twelve posts is retained, and the framing remains as before, with the exception that the one-story rear posts are replaced by two-story posts similar to those in the front wall, and the rear plate is placed at the same level as the front one. What was formerly the rear plate, in the house of but one room in depth, now becomes a second summer of the second story; and the two chimney girts of the second story, as well as the end girts, are extended until they meet the new rear plate. (Figure 48.)

Even in the house of central-hall plan, the fundamental framing scheme remains unchanged. The framing of a house of this type is in reality that of two houses of two-room plan placed side by side and connected by extensions of the sills and girts. As the two-room-plan houses have been turned at right angles to their former position, their second-story end girts now become the front and rear plates, and what were their plates become the end girts of the new arrangement. The summer beams, which appear to run from front to rear, in reality retain their old positions, and extend from the outside wall to the chimney.

Chapter IV. Roof Framing

TO the student of our early architecture, the framing of the roof is of importance scarcely secondary to that of the house itself. The two systems of framing are in fact so closely connected and so interdependent that it is often difficult to separate them. Nevertheless it is possible to classify the various modes of roof construction into several groups, each of which has its distinct characteristics.

In examining the house frame, we found that its construction was always or nearly always broadly similar. There were, to be sure, occasionally deviations from the general scheme, such as expressions of localism in the framing of joints; but on the whole the major members of the framework varied but little in size and arrangement. In the matter of roof construction, however, there is no corresponding uniformity. We do not find one general scheme followed throughout. The roof frame varied greatly in the details of its construction, and in several localities was radically different in system. Localism and individualism were more strongly accented in roof framing than in any other single feature of the early Connecticut house except the overhang.

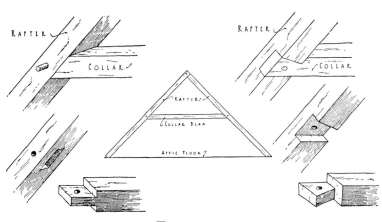

FIGURE 49.

Without doubt, the system of roof construction most frequently employed was that which made use of common rafters, with horizontal roof boarding. Even this simple arrangement may be divided into two usages: under one, collar beams were used; under the other, they were not. These variations were, as might be expected, regional. For instance, where a roof frame consists of a number of "common" rafters—*i.e.*, rafters all of the same size—spaced an equal distance on centers, the collar beam is to be expected and is generally found. It was used in order to prevent the rafters from sagging inward at their centers under the weight of the roof boards and shingles which they carried. (Figure 49.) In the New Haven Colony, however, the use of collar beams was the exception rather than the rule, and their absence is peculiar to that territory. From Figure 49 it may be seen that the collar beam was in reality the third member of a simple truss, and that it acted as a strut, or member in compression. This illustration shows the two general methods by

COWLES HOUSE—FARMINGTON

GAY MANSE—SUFFIELD

PITKIN HOUSE—EAST HARTFORD

GLEBE HOUSE—WOODBURY

PLATE VI.

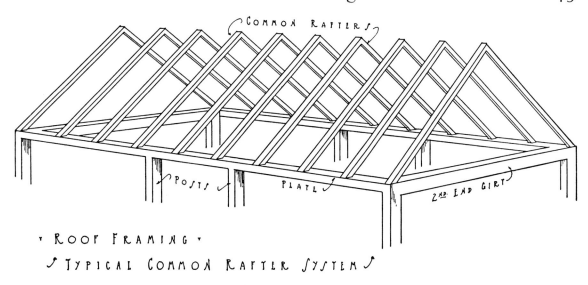

FIGURE 50.

which the collar was framed into the rafters. Of the two, the tusk-tenon-and-mortise joint is the more common, although the half-dovetail joint is to be met with rather frequently. These joints were nearly always secured by means of the inevitable wooden peg of about three-fourths inch diameter. Occasionally we find an example which proves the builder's realization that the peg was superfluous; that the combined weight of roof and rafters was more than sufficient to keep the collar beam in place, and that in no way could its tenon slip out of its mortise.

Where the roof frame consisted of a system of common rafters, the spacing was generally from three to four feet on centers, and all the rafters were alike. (Figure 50.) A great deal of variation is to be met with in the sectional dimensions of such rafters; in some instances the section is nearly square, in others it is rectangular. Rafters of square section usually measure about 5 by 5 inches to 6 by 6 inches; those of rectangular section 5 by 7 or 6 by 8 inches.

The more carefully built and finely finished houses have rafters which are broad-ax hewn; those of the

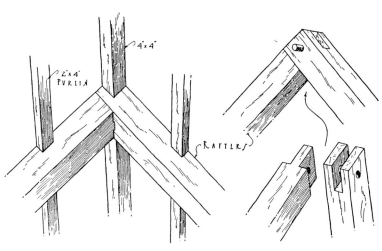

FIGURE 51.

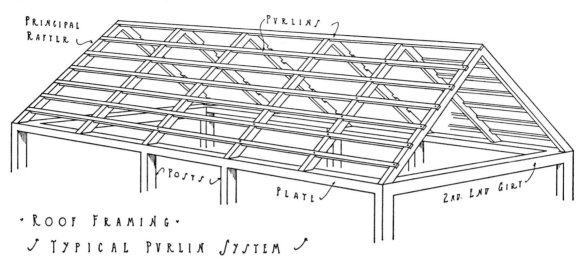

· ROOF FRAMING ·
✓ TYPICAL PURLIN SYSTEM ✓

FIGURE 52.

more crudely built houses may be simply rough poles, dressed on one side, and still retaining much of their original bark. Where rafters meet at the ridge, they are almost invariably framed together by means of the tenon joint, as shown in Figure 51. The ridgepole is never to be found except where it is part of a purlin system (Figure 52).

The common method of securing a footing for the rafters was by means of a double notch cut into the plates at their point of intersection. (Figure 53.) This double step provided a bearing for the rafter butt, which was further held in place by means of a peg of about one inch diameter, driven through it into the plate.

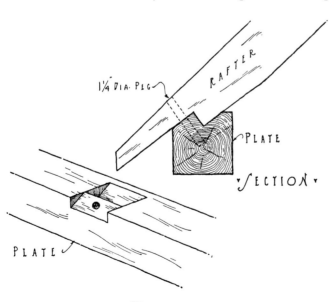

FIGURE 53.

The builders of the Guilford and Branford houses, and of those in the surrounding region, employed a totally different method of roof construction. These houses display, in nearly every example, roof frames made up of four, six, or eight pairs of heavy principal rafters, into which were framed horizontal purlins. These purlins, being horizontal, necessitated the use of vertical roof boarding, which extended up and down from ridge to plates, in the same direction as the rafters themselves.

Where the purlin system exists, a great deal of variation is to be found in the number, size, placing, and framing of these members. It is interesting to note that the influence of this framing system extended as far eastward as Saybrook, where an occasional house is to be found, the roof of which is built in this manner.

A typical system of purlin construction is to be seen in the roof of the Harrison-Linsley house in Branford (1690). (Figure 54.) This framework is made up of six pairs of principal rafters, which are of oak, hewn, and about 4½ by 6¾ inches in section. These principals are spaced about eight feet on centers, with the exception of those forming the central bay, which are nine feet on centers. Into these rafters are framed the purlins,

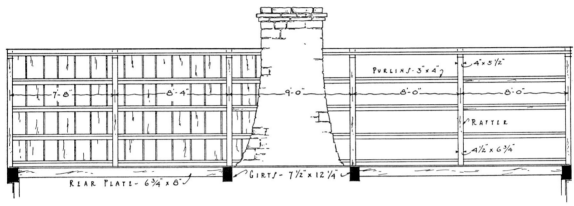

· Section Showing Roof Framing ·
Harrison-Linsley House - Branford
Figure 54.

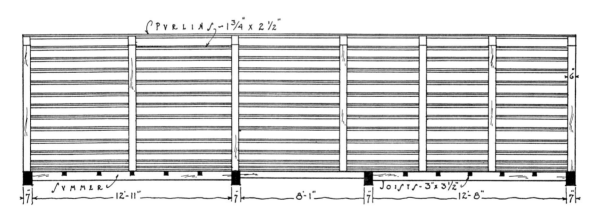

· Longitudinal Section Of Attic - Showing Framing ·
Moulthrop House - East Haven
Figure 55.

roughly 3 by 4 inches, three rows on the front, and the same number on the rear, with a single purlin at the peak, forming the ridge. These purlins, where they cross the rafters, are halved into them, and secured in addition by a wooden peg driven through the joint. The roof boarding, which is of wide oak boards, an inch thick, of course extends up and down from ridge to plates.

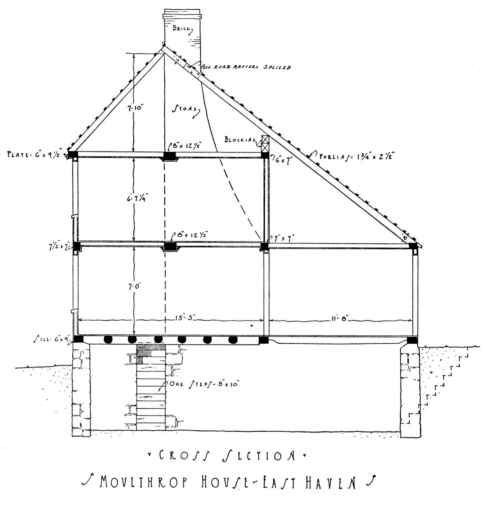

· CROSS SECTION ·
· MOULTHROP HOUSE-EAST HAVEN ·

FIGURE 56.

The roof of the Acadian house in Guilford (1670) is framed in quite the same manner, with the exception that there are six rows of purlins, front and rear, in addition to that at the ridge. The principal rafters are 4½ by 8 inches in section, and the purlins 2½ by 2¾ inches, framed flatwise into the rafters. (Figure 8.)

In the roof of the Moulthrop house in East Haven (demolished in 1919) there was to be seen a framing scheme of the utmost interest. (Figure 55.) Although made up of horizontal purlins and the usual rafters, this roof is not properly classifiable under the purlin system. It is rather to be regarded as a survival of the traditional use of thatch, for the small and closely spaced purlins were in reality nothing more or less than thatch poles. These purlins, which were approximately 1¾ by 2½ inches in section, and from 12 to 13 inches on centers, were spiked on to the rafters, and the shingles in turn nailed to them. Rafters and purlins were of oak, and the shingles of white pine, 2 feet 6 inches long, hand shaved. (Figure 56.)

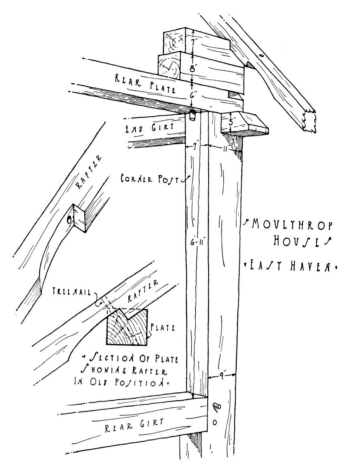

FIGURE 57.

In the framing of this roof, there is also written a novel bit of architectural history. From Figure 57 it may be seen that the rear or lean-to rafters have been raised out of the seats cut for them in the rear plate, and secured in a new position by means of oak blocks placed beneath them where they bear on the plate, and fifteen inches above it. In addition, each rear rafter has been lengthened about two feet by means of a new piece spliced on to its upper end. This blocking up and lengthening out of the rafters was made necessary by an increase in the depth of the lean-to rooms, which at some time in the history of the house must have been found necessary.

Another variation of the purlin system may be seen in the roof of the Bradley house in Branford (*circa* 1730). This roof is framed with four pairs of very heavy principal rafters, which, with their unusually large collar beams, really form four sturdy trusses. (Figure 58.) These trusses, if so they may be called, carry two heavy purlins, which are framed into them. Into these purlins, in turn, two small rafters are framed between each two pairs

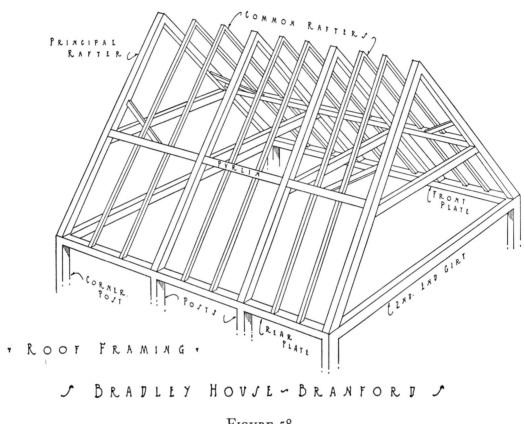

FIGURE 58.

of trusses. The principal rafters, or legs of the trusses, it should be observed, are two inches heavier at the butt than at their apex. The steep pitch of this roof should also be noted. The roof of the Morris house at Morris Cove, near New Haven, is framed in a similar manner.

A still different form of roof construction exists in the Bidwell-Mix house in West Hartford (1695-1700), and the older Williams house in Wethersfield (*circa* 1680). The framing of these two roofs is markedly similar, as may be seen from Figure 59. The system in each case consists of four pairs of principal rafters, measuring 4½ by 8 inches deep, of hewn oak, framed together at the ridge in the customary manner. A single horizontal purlin is framed in between every two rafters, and serves as a support for the smaller common rafters which bear upon it, and which are held in place by pegs. These smaller intermediate rafters are simply rough poles of about four inches' diameter, slightly flattened on the outer side. In both of these houses, the end sets of rafters are above the end girts, and the central pairs above the chimney girts. Rafter feet and girts therefore meet the plate at the same point. (Figure 34.)

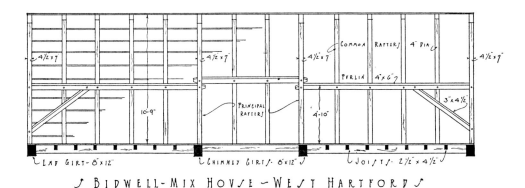

ʃ BIDWELL-MIX HOVʃE – WEʃT HARTFORD ʃ

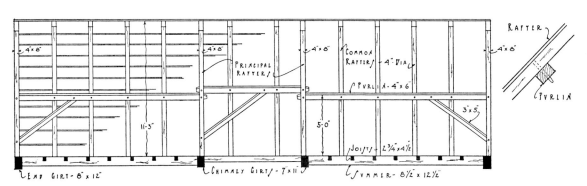

ʃ OLDER WILLIAMʃ HOVʃE – WETHERʃFIELD ʃ
· LONGITVDINAL ʃECTIONʃ OF ATTICʃ – ʃHOWING FRAMING ·

FIGURE 59.

It is obvious that in a house of the lean-to type the width of the lean-to on the first floor was determined by the pitch or angle of the rear rafters from the main house ridge to the rear plate. (Figure 6.) Extending downward from that point, their intersection with the first-floor ceiling joists determined the location of the lean-to plate. We have seen how a greater width of lean-to was secured, at considerable pains, by a rearrangement of the rear rafters of the Moulthrop house; let us see how the same problem was solved in other cases.

In Guilford, Branford, and the surrounding region we find a group of houses, of which the old Evarts Tavern of Northford (*circa* 1710) is typical, and in which the desired additional width of lean-to was secured by the use of a second rear plate, from 18 to 24 inches above the first rear plate. This second rear plate served in reality as a purlin, and simply afforded an intermediate bearing for the long lean-to rafters. (Figure 39.)

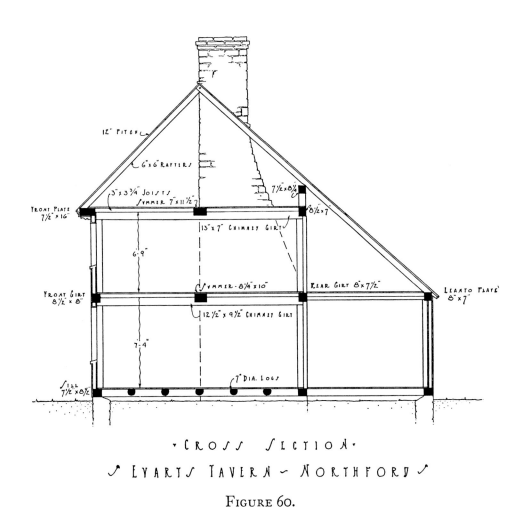

· C R O S S   S E C T I O N ·

· E V A R T S   T A V E R N ~ N O R T H F O R D ·

FIGURE 60.

The problem was met in a different way by the builder of the Deacon Stephen Hotchkiss house in Cheshire (*circa* 1730). This roof is framed with six pairs of heavy rafters, which increase in size toward their butts; into them are halved continuous 2 by 4 inch purlins, with a 4 by 4 inch purlin forming the ridge. (Figure 61.) Here lies the point of interest: to secure a greater span for the rear rafters, the ends of the girts, over which they occur, were cantilevered out beyond the rear plate, and tenoned into the rafters, which they sup-

STARKEY HOUSE—ESSEX

MORGAN HOUSE—CLINTON

HAWLEY HOUSE—RIDGEFIELD

OLD HOUSE—HARTFORD

PLATE VII.

ported. (Figure 61.) The second-story summers, however, instead of running from end girt to chimney girt in the usual manner, were turned at right angles and extended from front to rear plate, so that their cantilevered ends provided bearings for the two rafters, each of which was intermediate between the end and chimney girts. (Figure 62.) Similar construction is to be found in the Hall house, Cheshire (1730), where the two intermediate girts above mentioned appear as summers against the second-story ceilings, running parallel

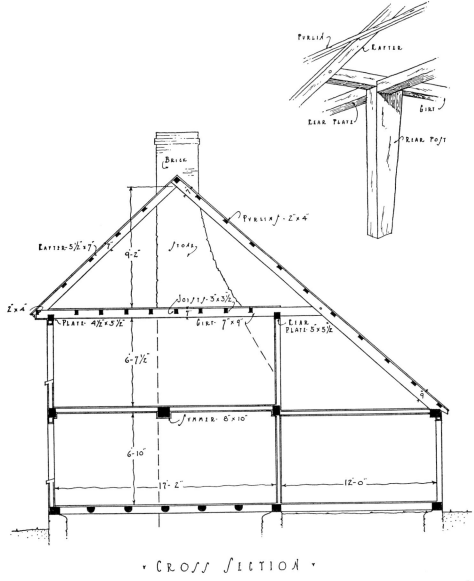

· CROSS SECTION ·
/ DEACON STEPHEN HOTCHKISS HOUSE ~ CHESHIRE /

FIGURE 61.

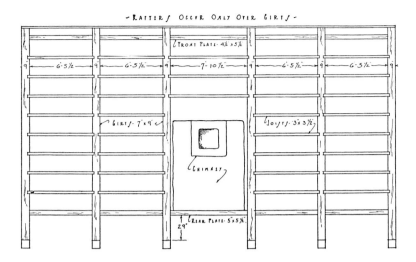

- RAFTERS OCCUR ONLY OVER GIRTS -

Front Plate - 4½ x 5½

9   6' - 5½   9   6' - 5½   9   7' - 10½   9   6' - 5½   9   6' - 5½   9

Girts - 7" x 9"   Joists - 3" x 3½"

Chimney

Rear Plate - 5" x 5½"

29"

• ATTIC FRAMING PLAN •
♪ DEACON STEPHEN HOTCHKISS • HOUSE ~ CHESHIRE ♪

FIGURE 62.

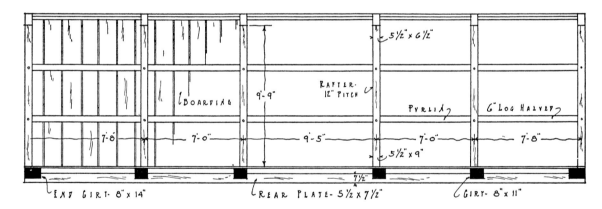

5½" x 6½"

Rafter -
12" Pitch

Boarding   9' - 9"   Purlin   6" Log Halved

7' - 8"   7' - 0"   9' - 5"   7' - 0"   7' - 8"

5½" x 9"

7½"

End Girt - 8" x 14"   Rear Plate - 5½ x 7½"   Girt - 8" x 11"

• LONGITUDINAL SECTION ~ OF ATTIC ~ SHOWING FRAMING •
♪ HALL HOUSE ~ CHESHIRE ♪

FIGURE 63.

with the ends of the house. These two beams are cased, and have handsomely panelled soffits. (Figures 63 and 64.)

This method of cantilever girt construction also appears as a characteristic of East Haven houses. The roof of the Bradley-Tyler house (*circa* 1745) is so framed (Figure 38), as is that of the Forbes or Barnes house (*circa* 1740). (Figure 65.) There is this difference,

FIGURE 64.

however: the Bradley-Tyler house roof is made up of six pairs of principal rafters, into which are framed light horizontal purlins; whereas the Forbes or Barnes house roof is constructed with ten pairs of common rafters, which require, besides the two end and two chimney girts, six additional intermediates to support them. These additional six girts take the place of the attic floor joists, and they are halved on to the front and rear plates, so that they finish flush with them, top and bottom. These six girts do not appear below the plastered ceiling of the second story, as do those in the Hall house. This method of cantilevered girt construction exists in the Benjamin house, Milford (*circa* 1750). I have not found it in any other localities than those mentioned. Although it may have been utilized to a considerable extent in those places, it cannot properly be called, on the whole, a common form of construction.

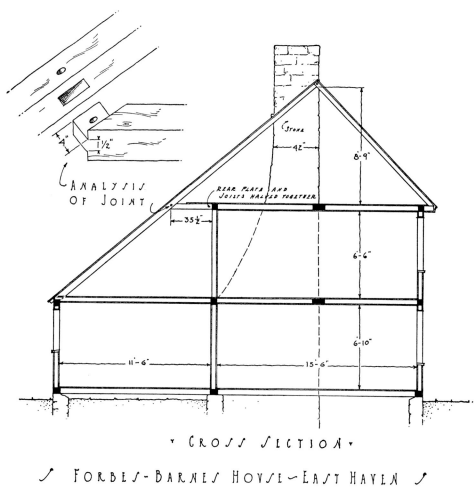

· CROSS SECTION ·

✎ FORBES-BARNES HOUSE—EAST HAVEN ✎

FIGURE 65.

This is the appropriate point at which to speak of the early roof pitch, or the angle at which the rafters were set. Undoubtedly, steepness was a characteristic of early roof construction. This tendency is easily explained by the fact that men who came from England were used to steeply pitched roofs, which were so built through actual necessity. English roof coverings were mainly of two sorts: thatch and slate. A thatch roof must be steep to shed water properly: and a slate roof must likewise be steep in order to transmute the great dead weight of the slates into a nearly vertical load upon the outside walls, rather than into an outward thrust, as would happen with a roof of flat pitch. We encounter here, once more then, the strong factor of tradition. There is every reason to believe that thatch was employed as the roofing material of the earliest houses, and that its use was discontinued only when it was found unsuited to the rigors and severe storms of our climate. The early

LEANTO FRAMING

·FORBES-BARNES HOUSE-EAST HAVEN·

FIGURE 66.

town records of Windsor mention the use of thatch as a roof covering of the church there; and if it were used for such a building, it is highly probable that it was used for houses as well. The early court records of New Haven also make mention of thatchers among the workmen present in the colony at that time. The Guilford records for the summer of 1651 ordered "the meeting house to be thatched and clayed before winter." Claying probably meant pointing the walls, which were of stone. As Atwater says: "The order to thatch shows that in Guilford, if not in other plantations, a thatched roof was thought worthy to cover the most honored edifices." Speaking of the first habitations erected in the New

Haven Colony, he says: "From the mention of thatchers, and the precautions taken against fire, it may be inferred that these humble tenements (log houses) were roofed with thatch." His inference is further strengthened by the existence of the office of chimney-viewer and by the frequent mention, in the early records of the colony, of the men who held it. According to the Hartford records it was the duty of the chimney-viewers to examine the chimneys every six weeks in winter, and every quarter in summer;

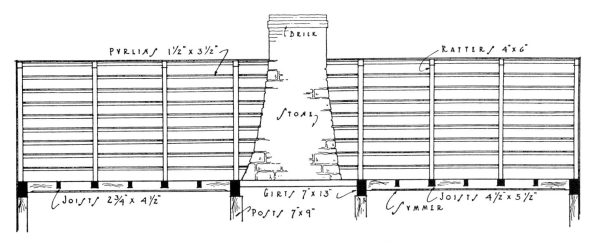

· SECTION SHOWING ATTIC FRAMING ·

S ALLEN SMITH HOVSE - MILFORD S

FIGURE 67.

and it is probable that the office very closely corresponds with that of the present-day fire-warden. It was, therefore, a post of importance and no mean responsibility, for in a way the safety of the community depended upon the vigilance of these men. "Chimney-viewers" were elected in Hartford until 1706.

The use of many small purlins, which may originally have been thatch poles, in constructing the roof of the Moulthrop house is also significant. Possibly this house had originally a thatched roof.

The drawing of the Governor Treat house, Milford, copied from one of Lambert's illustrations, shows a roof of extremely steep pitch. (Figure 68.) Even making allowance for exaggeration or faulty draftsmanship, the angle of the roof must have been very sharp. The Hempstead house of New London, the western part of which was built in 1643, is one of the earliest wooden houses standing to-day in the state of Connecticut. The pitch of the original roof of this house, as may be seen in the attic, where the old gable rafters are still in place, was fifteen inches to the foot, a very steep pitch. (Figure 69.) Mr. Ralph D. Smith, in information furnished Mr. Palfrey for his history, states that

WHITMAN HOUSE—FARMINGTON

HYLAND-WILDMAN HOUSE—GUILFORD

GLEASON HOUSE—FARMINGTON

HOLLISTER HOUSE—SOUTH GLASTONBURY

PLATE VIII.

The hip roof is characteristic of very late work, approaching 1800, or even later. It was never a common form of roof framing. The general scheme of construction is very similar to that of the gambrel roof, in that a single heavy horizontal purlin is framed upon posts rising from the second-story girts. This purlin, which is continuous and follows the four sides of the house, parallel with each in turn, forms the necessary support for the rafters of very flat pitch. With this type of roof, of which the Gay house, Suffield (1795), affords a good example, it should be noted that the second-story girts have become end plates, for the rafter feet bear upon them. Very rarely, as in the Prudence Crandall house, Canterbury (*circa* 1815), a hip roof made up of two pitches is to be found. Such a roof is really a combination of hip and gambrel. (Plate XXX.)

GAMBREL ROOF FRAMING

· GLEBE HOUSE-WOODBURY ·

FIGURE 71.

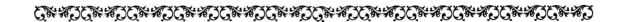

Chapter V. The Overhang

THE overhang is perhaps the most individual structural feature of the seventeenth-century Connecticut house. The overhang, as it is commonly referred to, is the projection of the second story beyond the first; and it usually occurred across the front of the house. Like many other characteristics of the earliest structures, the overhang was distinctly a survival of English tradition. It was a common feature of sixteenth- and seventeenth-century English town architecture. The purpose of the projecting stories or "jetties" was to provide protection from the weather to the stalls or booths which often existed beneath them on the ground floor.

The overhang, an extremely ancient form of construction, may be traced to a very remote origin. It even harks back to the days when Pompeii was a flourishing city. An edict of the Roman emperors forbade its use in narrow streets there, on the ground of its curtailment of sunlight and air.

Because the English overhang is chiefly to be found in the architecture of the towns and cities, seldom occurring in the country, we may reasonably expect to find it used in Connecticut in regions settled by craftsmen who originally came from towns and cities. The English overhang was always produced by framing, and was accordingly structural. In Connecticut, it remained of similar design up to 1675 or thereabout; for it was probably brought to American shores by the Yorkshire carpenters who emigrated to this country. In England the overhang occurred across the front of the house, which stood with its gable end toward the street. It is worthy of note that in Connecticut the tradition of constructing the overhang across the front was retained, although the house was turned so that its gable ends no longer faced the street or road upon which it stood. A framed overhang at the ends of the house was not common in Connecticut, and the projection was never greater than four or six inches. No form of overhang framing ever occurred at the rear of the house.

From Figure 27 a clear idea may be gained of the manner in which the framed overhang was constructed. It will be seen that the posts were but a single story in height, and that the second-story posts were framed out upon the projecting ends of chimney and end girts. Into these second-story posts a second front girt was framed. The system of double first-story front girts is therefore typical of the framed overhang. The projection of the second story beyond the first was generally in the neighborhood of two feet, which it never exceeded, though in some cases it was less. It should be noted that the framed overhang did not occur in towns lying outside the Connecticut River Valley, and that it never existed in the New Haven Colony.

In its earliest form the overhang was embellished on its under side with ornamental pendants or "drops," which served as terminations to the lower ends of the front second-

WHITMAN HOUSE—FARMINGTON

OLDER COWLES HOUSE—FARMINGTON

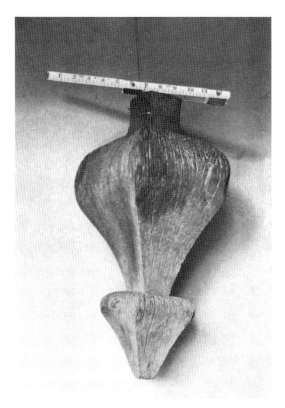

FROM A DEMOLISHED HOUSE—FARMINGTON

MOORE HOUSE—WINDSOR

PLATE IX.

story posts. There were thus four drops across the front of the house. (Figure 72.) These drops, which were hewn or worked out of the lower ends of the posts, of which they were an integral part, were of pleasing contour, and gave a decidedly piquant charm to the houses they adorned. Aside from the one example of chamfered girts, to be seen on the front of the Hyland-Wildman house, their use is the only instance of decorative treatment of structural forms in connection with the Connecticut house exterior.

FIGURE 72.

During the first stage the drops were sometimes supplemented by heavy brackets, purely ornamental and serving no structural purpose. The overhang treatment of the Cowles house (1650-1660) and the Gleason house (1650-1660) in Farmington is typical of this arrangement. The gable ends of the latter house project as well, and originally had two brackets at each end.

In the second stage the drops were retained, although the brackets behind them were discarded. The Moore house in Windsor (1664) and the Whitman house in Farmington (*circa* 1660) furnish us with examples of this phase. The Moore house still retains the brackets at one gable end, and it is not probable that the Whitman house ever had any. The drops of the Moore house, it is of considerable interest to note, are almost identical in form with those on a seventeenth-century house still standing in Hereford, England. One of the Moore house drops is shown in Plate IX. It will be seen from this illustration that the drop, though of curved contour, was four-sided. In this it is typical, for the rectangular form of the post above was always carried out in the pendant beneath it.

During the last quarter of the seventeenth century the overhang, retained as an outward form, though of much diminished projection, underwent a radical change in its construction. It was produced no longer by framing, but rather by hewing away the lower ends of the front posts, which became one continuous timber throughout their height. From Figure 27 it will be seen that, because of this diminution in size at the first story, the exterior face of the posts projected in the second story. The overhang was thus reduced from feet to inches. When of this form, the overhang is said to be of the "hewn" type, and it became as common as the framed type is rare.

It is evident that in Connecticut there were two schools of overhang construction: one which abruptly dropped the overhang before 1700; the other which retained it, though in much diminished form, until after 1775. The hewn type is, then, a descendant of the framed form—an American variation, structurally indigenous to this country. It is difficult to find any evidence which will establish definitely when the hewn overhang first came into use. Inasmuch as it occurred commonly in the New Haven Colony and lingered on until, or after, 1700, its use there was plainly an affectation; for it could claim no descent from the framed form, which had never existed in that locality.

When the overhang was of the hewn type, the tops of the posts were occasionally left exposed, just beneath the projection of the second story, and cut in the form of supporting corbels. Such treatment is rather rare; the Hollister house in Glastonbury (*circa* 1680) and the Caldwell house in Guilford (*circa* 1740) are two examples. (Plate X.) Unfortunately the corbels of the Hollister house do not appear as they did originally; for the house, in modern times, has been furred on the outside and given an additional covering of clapboards which partly covers this interesting construction, once entirely visible.

A variation of this corbel form of treatment occurs on the front of the Hyland-Wildman house in Guilford (*circa* 1660), where, in addition to the hewn corbels of the front posts, the first-story girts, handsomely chamfered with a bold moulding, are likewise exposed. (Plate X.) Such construction as this is decidedly unusual in Connecticut.

The hewn overhang, which is never more than six inches, and was commonly but three or four, usually extended across the front of the house and on either end; later it appeared on the rear as well. It gradually dwindled until it was little more than an inch in projection, and finally, during the last quarter of the eighteenth century, disappeared altogether. It is a feature to be associated almost entirely with the central-chimney type of house, and it was the last lingering expression of seventeenth-century quaintness to be visible on the exterior of the Conecticut house. Its disappearance was brought about by the advent of the stately and formal houses of the central-hall type of plan, which echoed the comparative sophistication of the period which produced them.

The persistence of the overhang, the tenacity with which it endured as a form of construction, is remarkable, especially if we stop to consider that, from a beginning based upon tradition pure and simple, it held sway through a period of nearly a hundred and fifty years.

GLEASON HOUSE—FARMINGTON

CALDWELL HOUSE—GUILFORD

HYLAND-WILDMAN HOUSE—GUILFORD

HOLLISTER HOUSE—SOUTH GLASTONBURY

PLATE X.

Chapter VI. The Summer

OF the numerous timbers which make up the framework of the early Connecticut house, none plays a more prominent part than the summer. It was not only important structurally, but its exposed position helped to give it an added interest which other members, concealed from view, did not possess.

The summer is an old form of construction, and, like its English prototype, almost invariably extended from the outside wall across the room to the chimney. It is a regular feature of English work of the period under discussion. The cottage plan shown in Figure 73 indicates it in its customary position.

In Connecticut the summer beams were placed parallel with the front of the house. Examples are rare in which the summer runs in the opposite direction—that is, parallel with the chimney girts, from front to rear of the house. This arrangement, to be sure, does occur in the original part of the Hempstead house in New London (1643), the east front room of the Graves house in Madison (1675), and the Allyn house in Windsor (*circa* 1750). But this last house, which is of brick construction, can hardly be cited as an example, for it does not properly come under the head of timber construction. A combination of

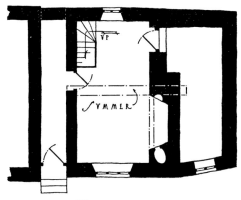

FIGURE 73.

the two systems is to be seen in the Moore house in Windsor (1664). In this house, originally of two-room plan, each room had two summers, which were curiously crossed at the center. By exception to the usual rule, the summers in this house are not of oak, but of a native variety of hard pine. Curiously, both the Hempstead and the Graves houses, which have summers extending from front to rear in the rooms on one side of the chimney, display, in the other front rooms on the opposite side of the chimney, two summers parallel to each other and to the front of the house. (Figures 9 and 11.)

As I stated in the chapter on framing, the ends of the summer, when it is in its conventional position, were framed into the end girt and the chimney girt by means of a dovetail joint. (Figure 35.) The advantage of such construction lay in the fact that the summer could not sag beneath the floor loads transmitted to it through the joists, unless it first gave way at the ends.

From the numerous illustrations of houses shown in cross section, it will be seen that in nearly every instance a second summer at the attic-floor level repeated that below it at the second-floor level. In framing and purpose it was identical with the one beneath it; and it was generally of the same size. Exceptions to this customary arrangement exist in many of the Stratford and Milford houses which are still standing to-day; for, while the second-floor summers occupy their usual exposed position against the ceilings of the first floor, no summer is visible in the second story. There is reason to believe that, in some cases, these second summers exist, though in reduced form; for two parallel cracks often indicate the presence of this beam beneath the plastering.

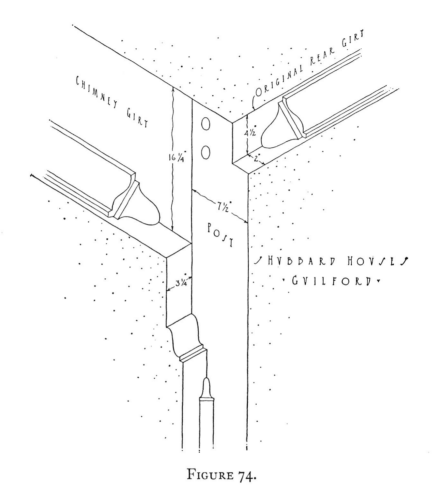

FIGURE 74.

The vertical dimension or depth of the summer varied at different periods, but its width was usually in the neighborhood of twelve inches. The summer beams in the Allen Smith house in Milford (*circa* 1690) display the tremendous width of 17½ inches; those of the Eri Bradley house in North Haven (*circa* 1730) measure but a half inch less. Both of these examples are unusually heavy; in fact, the entire framing of the Smith house is almost barbaric in its weight and massive crudeness.

In early work, before the introduction of plastering, the summer, as well as the joists which were framed into it, was left exposed on the under side, being covered above by

WELLES-SHIPMAN HOUSE—SOUTH GLASTONBURY

WHITFIELD HOUSE—GUILFORD

COLONEL HITCHCOCK HOUSE—CHESHIRE

HART HOUSE—SAYBROOK

PLATE XI.

the floor which was laid over it. Where the summers were never cased or plastered over, the marks of the broad-ax are nearly always plainly visible, there having been, except for a slight chamfering of the lower corners, no further attempt at finishing.

The chamfering is a characteristic treatment of the summer. It varies in different examples from a simple bevelling to a handsomely moulded finish, such as is to be seen in the Hubbard house in Guilford (1717). (Figure 74.) Very curiously, the chamfering of the summer beams of the Hubbard house is almost identical in section with that of the first-story front girts of the Hyland-Wildman house (*circa* 1660) in the same town, as may be seen from the exterior. (Plate X.) It is quite probable that both are the handiwork of the same craftsman. Such elaborate chamfering as this example exhibits is, however, unique. The boldness of its section makes it of exceptional interest. When the chamfer was of simpler form, much pleasing ingenuity was exercised in the manner of its termination at either end. The terminations or "chamfer stops," as they were commonly styled, were for the purpose of preventing the chamfering from running into the girts into which the summer was dovetailed at either end. (Figure 75.)

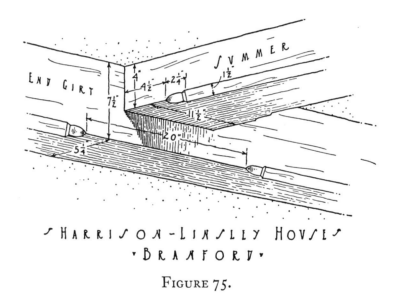

SHARRISON-LINSLLY HOVSES
·BRANFORD·

FIGURE 75.

Plastering, which was absent from most of the earliest houses, brought about the casing of structural members, including the summer, which had formerly been exposed on the inside of the house. In fact, the use of plaster as a means of interior finish sounded the signal for the disappearance of the summer. This is especially true of the first floor, where plaster was first used; so that very often the summer does not appear exposed on the first floor, although it was retained on the second. Such an arrangement exists in the Caldwell house in Guilford (*circa* 1740). The use of the exposed summer in this way, on only the second floor, continued up to about 1750, after which time it was abandoned altogether. Probably because of the early use of plaster in the New Haven Colony, the omission of the summer, especially on the first floor, occurred there earlier than elsewhere. In other Connecticut settlements, the first- and second-story summers generally disappeared simultaneously; although in Milford and Stratford a number of houses exist in which the summers show as described above, only in the first story.

In many instances the summer persisted even after the advent of plastering. It was then made less in depth; so that it became concealed by the ceiling beneath it, although it still carried the ends of the joists as formerly. Where this arrangement exists, the presence of the summer may usually be detected by two tell-tale parallel cracks in the plaster, due to shrinkage or settlement.

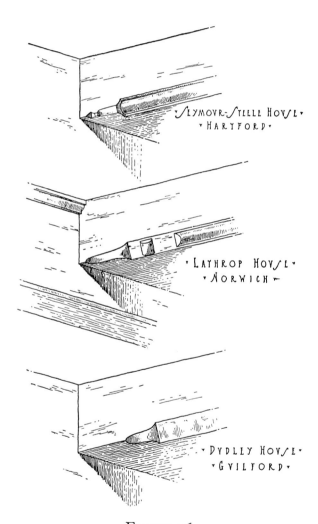

FIGURE 76.

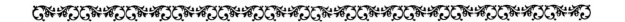

Chapter VII. Masonry

TO recur once more to the subject of tradition, we find that the small English house of the period under consideration was built, practically always, without a cellar beneath it. In fact, this usage still persists in England. It is not surprising, then, to find under the earliest Connecticut houses cellars which extend beneath only a part of the structures above them. Often there was no direct communication between the cellar and the house itself, the entrance to the cellar being through an outside door or "hatchway" on the southern or more sheltered end of the house. Where this arrangement existed, the cellar is usually to be found beneath the hall or living room, which was always on the warmer side of the house. The Cyrus Hawley house, in Monroe, built about 1740, has such a cellar. It extends only beneath the living room, on the southern side of the house, and access to it is by means of an outside flight of stone steps down from grade to a door through the cellar wall. It is inaccessible from the interior of the house.

The difficulty of excavating large and deep cellars must have been an important factor at first. That it was so is proved, indeed, not only by the fact that the excavation was but partial, but also by the fact that the early cellars were very shallow. The cellar bottom was, most often, simply of earth. Stone flagging or paving was evidently never popular in Connecticut. Where it does occur, it is as a part of late work; it rarely appears in houses built before the last quarter of the eighteenth century. Examples of such flagging may be seen in the cellar of the Miner Fowler house in Guilford, built 1765, and in that of the Barnabas Deane house in Hartford, built in 1778.

The cellar or foundation walls, as well as the substructure of the chimney stack, were invariably of stone. Material secured in the vicinity was nearly always employed; ordinary field stone appears to have been most commonly used. It was only in rare instances, or at a comparatively late date, that quarried stone was used in walls below grade. The marks of actual quarrying on cellar stones is extremely unusual. Such quarried stones were usually roughly split blocks of gneiss or stratified granite, taken from the outcropping ledges which are so common about Guilford and Norwich. The earliest evidence of such quarrying exists in the cellar of the Hempstead house in New London, which was begun in 1643. From old records it appears that the quarrying of the abundant red sandstone in the region about Hartford was carried on at an early date. Stones used for foundation walls, then, were of two sorts, field and quarry; and the choice of material depended upon what the neighborhood had to offer.

The foundation walls in the cellars of some houses contain a niche or recess of 10 or 12 inches in depth, and 18 inches or 2 feet in width and height. Sometimes the recess occurs in the chimney foundation. It was evidently incorporated to provide a cool place for food or preserves during the warmer months, though possibly it may have served some other purpose.

The foundation walls of rough field stone, or split gneiss, were at first either "laid up dry"—that is, without mortar of any sort—or with clay as a substitute for mortar. This practice was probably due to the scarcity of lime and the difficulty of getting it. In the southern part of the state, and especially in towns situated near the Sound, where oyster shells were easily obtained and burned to produce lime, the use of regular mortar in the construction of masonry was earlier and more common. The masonry ends of that part of the Morris house at Morris Cove, near New Haven, which constitutes the original building (1670) are built of stones laid in mortar, the lime of which was obtained from oyster shells.

Lime was used very early in New London and New Haven, and the records of the latter town for November 3, 1639, refer to it as follows: "It is ordered that Mr. Hopkins shall have two hogsheads of lime for his present use, and as much more as will finish his house as he now intends it." In 1640 these records mention carting lime from the waterfront, from which we may infer that it was in use at that time, although produced elsewhere. A court order for June 11, 1640, fixed the price of lime as follows: "Lime well burnt un-slaked, and brought by water to the landing-place of the town, by the bushell heaped, not above 9d. the bushell."

Whether lime was ever brought from England is a point open to question; I personally doubt it. The early court records of New Haven repeatedly refer to the "oyster shell field," which was situated east of State Street, between Chapel and George. It was probably an Indian refuse heap, similar to the extensive one still in existence at Lighthouse Point, near New Haven. Certainly oyster shells were abundant; and, with such a supply of raw material at hand, it is improbable that the importation of lime was ever resorted to, especially since we find oyster-shell lime to have been a component of the mortar in very early work.

Throughout the state, clay was used, in the majority of cases, as a substitute for mortar in the construction of the massive stone chimney stacks. It was employed to fill the joints throughout the chimney's* height and up to its point of emergence through the roof. Above the roof, lime mortar was used, for rain would quickly have washed the clay out of the exposed joints. The remarkably good condition to-day of work in the construction of which clay was used originally, is due, no doubt, more to the careful bonding of the stonework and its general massiveness than to any virtue of the clay as a mortar. Some consideration must be given to the fact, however, that the heat of fires maintained, some of them, for two hundred years has done much to bake or harden this substitute for mortar.

Owing to the custom of keeping the first-floor level close to grade, the height of exposed underpinning between the earth and the sills was never great. Even in early work, if the house were high enough above grade to expose the underpinning, a rough attempt was generally made to dress the stone blocks to regular shape and to lay them in courses.

* It should be noted that in early times "chimney" meant flue, whereas the word "chimney," as we use it to-day, meant stack.

BARTLETT HOUSE—GUILFORD

GRISWOLD HOUSE—GUILFORD

OSBORN HOUSE—SOUTHPORT

SHELTON HOUSE—STRATFORD

PLATE XII.

Generally this treatment occurred only across the front of the house, the underpinning of the other three walls being left rough. In very late work, regular blocks of carefully dressed red Portland sandstone were commonly used for the underpinning. Brick was occasionally used for this purpose in the construction of late houses, but rarely before the first half of the eighteenth century. Brick underpinning may be regarded as, on the whole, unusual, regular quarried stone having been employed in preference. The earliest instance of the use of brick for underpinning, so far as is known, is the Meggatt house in Wethersfield, built in 1730. The underpinning of the Burrage Merriam house in Rocky Hill (*circa* 1760) is of brick, the individual measurements of which are 7 by 1¾ by 3⅜ inches.

From Revolutionary times onward the underpinning received much attention. In most of the houses it was well and carefully built, and material for its construction was often brought from considerable distances. A typical stone from the underpinning of the Orton house, built in Farmington about 1698, and now demolished, is shown in Figure 77. The material is a variety of conglomerate sandstone, and its measurements are 7 feet 3 inches in length by 1 foot in height. The exposed face of the stone has been cut with false joints of V-shaped section, which subdivide it into a number of rectangular blocks.

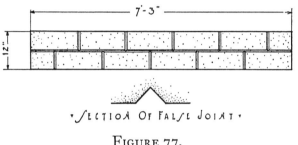

· SECTION OF FALSE JOINT ·

FIGURE 77.

The most important piece of masonry in connection with the house, was, of course, the chimney stack. The amount of stone used in its construction was very great, and the sheer mass of this tremendous pile of masonry is astounding, when as has sometimes happened, the house has collapsed and the chimney stack remains standing, a monument to mark its site. (Plate XV.) The massive chimney stack is especially characteristic of the central-chimney houses, the builders of which used stone with lavish hands. After the transition to the central-hall or two-chimney plan, the mass of the chimney stacks became comparatively much smaller. More imposing in size than even the stack of the chimney at the first-floor level was its foundation in the cellar. Chimney foundations 10 and 12 feet square, and even larger, are not uncommon. The upper part of the foundation was often corbelled out to provide a bearing, not only for the hearthstones above, but also for the timbers extending from the front to the rear sills, into which the first-floor joists were framed. (Plate XIV.)

Occasional chimney foundations are found, such as those in the Ripley house in South Coventry (1792), which contain a large vault-like space. The opening to each of these spaces (there is one in each chimney, the house being of central-hall plan), is just above the cellar bottom, and about eighteen inches square. The chimney foundations of the Grant house in Windsor (1757-1758) were traversed by a barrel vault, built of brick, and extending from front to rear. This is a rare feature. A somewhat similar arrangement of chimney

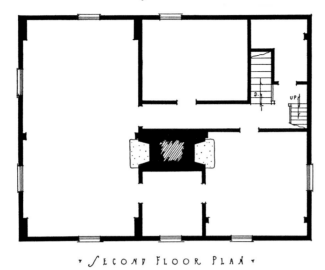

· SECOND FLOOR PLAN ·

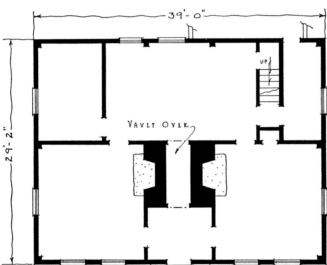

· FIRST FLOOR PLAN ·

∫ CAPTAIN JOHNSON HOUSE—HAMBURG ∫

FIGURE 78.

vaulting existed in the Tuttle house in West Hartford (*circa* 1700) until recent years, and may still be seen in the Captain Johnson house in Hamburg (1790). Each of these houses is of central-chimney plan, with the chimney divided on the first floor so that a fireplace occurs in each front room. By means of a barrel vault at the height of the first-floor ceiling, the two flues were brought together, and from that point continued upward as a single stack. (Figure 78.) In the Tuttle house, this space in the chimney was occupied by the stairs to the second floor.

In some instances chimney stacks were constructed of stone up to the second-floor level, and from that point carried up in brick. The chimney of the Bradley-Tyler house in East Haven (*circa* 1745) is an example of this construction. More commonly, the stack was built of stone up to the attic-floor level or to the under side of the roof, and "topped out" with brick. In many instances the brick above the roof replaced an earlier termination of stone. A characteristic of chimney construction of the central-hall type of house is the use of stone up to the level of the attic floor, above which the stack is built of brick, often simply laid in clay.

The treatment of a chimney above the roof with pilaster-like projections, such as are to be seen frequently in Rhode Island and Massachusetts work, seldom occurred in Connecticut. (Plate XII.) Some old drawings of the old tavern kept by Moses Butler at the corner of Main and Elm Streets and of the Saunders house which stood on Charter Oak Avenue, in Hartford, do, however, show a treatment of this sort. The use of one or more "saw-tooth"

HALE HOUSE—SOUTH GLASTONBURY

COLONEL BARKER HOUSE—NORTH HAVEN

WEBSTER HOUSE—EAST WINDSOR

CHAFFEE HOUSE—WINDSOR

PLATE XIII.

courses, formed by setting the brick diagonally with one corner exposed, is occasionally to be seen, though it is a rare feature. The Talcott house which stood in Glastonbury is probably the only example of the use of the saw-tooth course projecting from the face of the chimney without a projecting brick course above and below it.

It is probable that in the early days of the colony some chimneys were constructed of logs laid crosswise, or "cob fashion," or of wattles. Such chimneys, even though thickly plastered on the inside with clay, were dangerous, and necessitated the most scrupulous attention by the "chimney-viewers." The Hartford records of 1639 mention chimneys of clay as well as of brick; so that there can be no question as to the existence of clay chimneys.

In the earliest houses the center of the stack was invariably carried up *behind* the main roof ridge, and the chimney was long and narrow, its length being parallel with the ridge.

The small oval-shaped bake ovens built in connection with the kitchen fireplace (or that of the hall, if the house were of two-room plan) were generally constructed of brick, even when the rest of the chimney was built of stone. This use of brick may be due to the fact that such ovens were often built in at a date later than that of the chimney itself. The floor of the oven was usually placed at a height of about three feet from the floor, and the oven itself measured approximately 30 inches in depth by 18 inches in width, though examples occur which are much larger. These ovens were domed over with brick— a piece of construction which was always very nicely executed. The floors were sometimes of brick also, but more often they were formed by single slabs of stone. Beneath the oven is usually found a recessed chamber, built into the chimney stack, probably for the storage of cooking utensils or wood. (Plate XXXVIII.) As these ovens had no connection with the chimney flues, they were used for baking by filling them with glowing wood embers from the adjoining fireplace. After the walls had become thoroughly heated the coals were raked out, and the food to be baked was placed inside. The opening was then tightly closed and the oven left to do its work, on much the same principle as the modern "fireless cooker."

Like its English prototype, the fireplace of the early Connecticut house was of generous proportions. Depended upon for heat as well as for cooking, it was naturally the center of domestic life, "the warm heart whose glow cheered the household." The largest fireplace in the house was usually that of the kitchen, when the house was of the lean-to type. That of the Welles-Shipman house in Glastonbury (1750) measures 9 feet 5 inches in width by 4 feet 6 inches in height. It is three feet deep and contains two brick ovens. The kitchen fireplace of the Freeman Curtis house in Stratford (1710) is 7 feet 7 inches wide by 3 feet 8 inches high. The hall fireplace of the Buckingham house in Milford, which is said to have been built in 1639, measured, before the addition of a brick oven at one end, 7 feet 8 inches in width by 3 feet 9 inches in height; and that of the Hyland-Wildman house in Guilford (*circa* 1660) 8 feet 5 inches in width by 3 feet 10 inches in height. These large fireplaces are invariably built of roughly dressed stone, brick construction indicating work of a later date. The other fireplaces of the first floor (there is always one in each front room) were smaller, and the dimensions of those on the second floor were still less. It is not at all unusual to find one of the front chambers of the second floor, where the house is of central-chimney plan, without a fireplace; and a fireplace in the "kitchen chamber" is rather the exception than the rule.

The cellar fireplace is an extremely rare feature, but it does occasionally occur. The Martin Page house in Branford (*circa* 1750) and the Danforth house in Rocky Hill (*circa* 1770), both of central-chimney plan, have fireplaces in their cellars. The Captain Charles

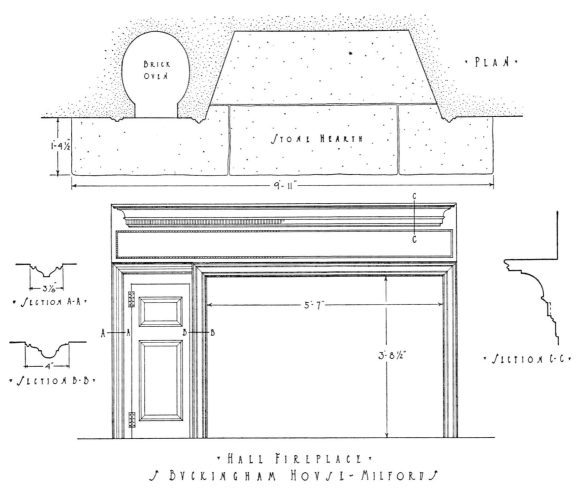

FIGURE 79.

Churchill house (1763), which stood in Newington, contained an immense fireplace in the cellar, built into the central chimney. This fireplace was of such ample dimensions that it was possible, according to tradition, to roast a whole ox therein at one time. A cellar fireplace of very large size also exists in the Joel Bradley house in North Haven (1759).

A great many fireplaces of small dimensions are the result of work done later than the original house-building; and this is especially true of small fireplaces with brick sides. For various reasons the original fireplace was at some time considered to be too large, and its size was accordingly reduced by the construction of a new back and sides, the original height generally being retained. Such changes often took place at the time when the fireplace walls were panelled.

Where all the fireplaces were constructed at the same time, it was customary, so far as is known, to carry up the flue of each so that all met or emerged into a common flue in the upper part of the chimney. All the flues were large, but no form of flue lining was ever employed. The chimney of the Captain Charles Churchill house in Newington (1763) was of unusual construction, so a descendant of the family states, in that it contained no less than seven flues, each of which was carried up to the top independently of the others. Mr. Sheldon Thorpe of North Haven states that each of the end chimneys of the Joel Bradley house in that town (1759) has two or three separate flues.

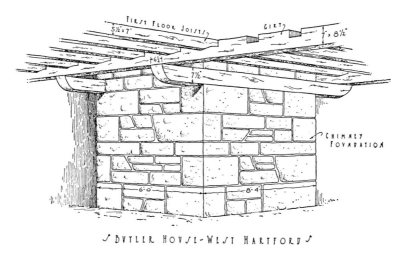

BUTLER HOUSE—WEST HARTFORD

FIGURE 80.

Stone was generally used in building the sides and back of the fireplace; but the parlor fireplace was often faced with common red brick. It was not until about 1800 that the use of brick for all the fireplaces became general. When the fireplace opening was of too great a width to be conveniently spanned by a stone lintel, a squared timber of oak was used instead. In regions where stone was scarce or difficult to quarry, such oak lintels were used even for small openings. Wood lintels were often very heavy; for instance, that in the kitchen of the "White Farm" at Long Ridge measures 17½ inches deep by 10 inches wide. Those in the older Bushnell house in Saybrook (1678-1679) are 15 inches deep by 12 inches wide. Where wood was so employed, its height above the hearth seems usually to have been sufficient to protect it from taking fire. Where the lintel of the fireplace was of stone, the ends were often placed upon templates or bearing blocks of wood. The reason for this measure is not clear, unless it was to prevent the lintel from rolling or changing its position during any possible settlement of the chimney subsequently to its construction. The fact that these bearing timbers of the fireplace lintel are often continued right through the chimney, to serve a similar purpose on the opposite side, rather indicates that this was actually the purpose of such an arrangement.

Heavy hewn timbers, sometimes with mortise holes, or the marks of having been previously used in the construction of an older building, are often to be found built into the cellar foundations of stone chimneys. The purpose of the builders in using this device was undoubtedly to secure a better bond, the large timbers serving to tie the whole mass of stonework more firmly together.

The front and back hearths were most often of flat stone slabs, one piece serving for each. The front hearth, which finished level with the wood floor, is always of greater width on the first than on the second floor—a fact explained by the support afforded the first-floor hearth by the foundations of the chimney in the cellar below. It was customary to corbel or build out the base of the chimney stack in order not only to carry the hearth-stones of the first floor, but also to provide a support for the cellar chimney girts.

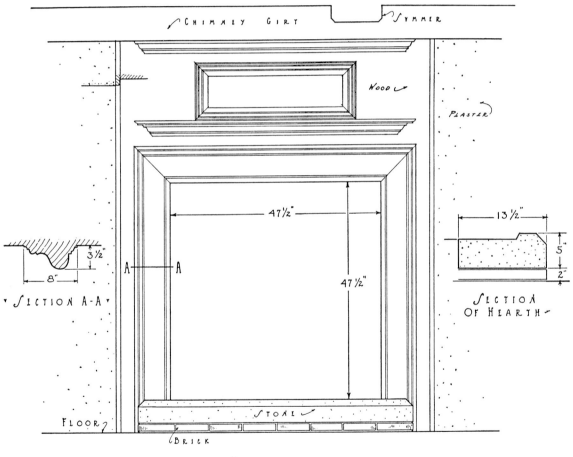

· FIREPLACE ·

/ OLDER WILLIAMS HOVSE ~ WETHERSFIELD /

FIGURE 81.

The use of brick or square tile for hearth construction appears to have been unusual; at any rate, it is a late usage. Brick hearths do occur where stone fireplaces have been narrowed and new brick ovens built in, as in the halls of two-room-plan houses, and in the kitchens of houses of the lean-to type.

An unusual instance on record involves the employment of an old tombstone, with the inscription side up, as a hearth stone. The house was that built by Captain Charles Churchill in Newington in 1763 (now demolished). This odd hearth was that of the fireplace in the second-floor kitchen chamber. One of the second-story fireplaces of the older Williams house in Wethersfield, built *circa* 1680, has a very curious form of hearth. (Figure 81.) It is cut from a single piece of brownstone or "Portland Stone," and its top is raised above the floor a distance of seven inches. A bevel-edged rim prevented coals or ashes from dropping off on to the wooden floor.

It was not until the latter half of the eighteenth century that colored glazed tiles, usually of Dutch origin, were made use of for facing the fireplace opening. They were never commonly used in Connecticut; and often they are a later addition. It is only in the more elaborate and finely built houses that we find the fireplaces framed by moulded

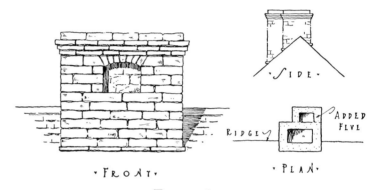

FIGURE 82.

stone architraves, as in the parlor of the Silas Deane house in Wethersfield, built 1764. (Plate XXXIV.) A much simpler form of stone architrave is that of the parlor fireplace of the Henry Deming house, Wethersfield, built 1790, which consists of several moulded members and an incised conventional pattern of ornament. (Figure 170.) The use of marble as a facing is not to be expected save in extremely late houses, dating after 1800.

As all the cooking of the earlier houses was done at the fireplaces, the wrought-iron crane, with its dependencies of pot-hooks and trammels, is generally found, in hall and kitchen fireplaces, supported by two iron eyes fastened into the masonry at one side. An earlier arrangement is the simple bar of iron built into the masonry at each end, from which pots and kettles were hung.

Another feature in connection with the chimney stack is the smoke chamber or "smoke oven" found in the attic—an ingenious arrangement by means of which the smoke ascending the chimney flues was utilized for curing meats. For safety's sake, the door to the chamber was usually made of sheet iron. The smoke chamber is not an early feature, and it is generally found only in the more elaborate houses.

The chimney top of the General Walker house in Stratford, built about 1740, is shown in Figure 82. A recessed niche about 18 inches square and three or four inches deep was built into the stonework on the front side, and traces of plaster or stucco still clinging to the stones show that it was carefully finished on the inside, for some purpose or other—possibly so that the family arms or the date of building could be painted on it.

Since flashing was not employed by the early builders as we use it to-day, it was necessary to resort to some other expedient in order to make a water-tight joint between the roof and the chimney. This was done by projecting a thin course of stone, or a course of brick, for a distance of about three inches just above the point of intersection with the roof, so that the shingles could be tucked underneath. This measure proved fairly rain-proof.

In sectional plan above the roof line, the oldest chimneys were long and narrow, the long axis being parallel with the ridge. The later chimneys became more nearly square, but the mass of the chimney stack still generally remained behind the ridge.

When the original house was of two-room plan and a lean-to containing a kitchen was added, a new flue was made necessary. Such additions to the chimney stack are always easily traced, especially as the work was often very clumsily done. The chimney, where it appeared above the roof, became L- or T-shaped in plan—one of the surest indications that the lean-to, where it exists, was a later addition. (Figure 82.)

From available evidence it is clear that the use of brick in chimney building began to appear during the last quarter of the seventeenth century, in New Haven and Hartford. In remote places where brick were not manufactured or readily obtainable, the use of stone persisted until late. In localities such as Guilford and Norwich, for example, where stone was plentiful, brick never became popular for chimney building.

Old records show that brick were manufactured at a very early date both in Hartford and New Haven, and there is some reason to believe that they were imported into New Haven. Atwater mentions a brickmaker in his list of "house-holders" of New Haven during 1641-1643. Brick were made, soon after the founding of the colony, from the clay underlying the Quinnipiac marshes; for Theophilus Eaton's brickyard at "East Farms" (now Cedar Hill) was transferred at his death in 1658 to Thomas Yale. The New Haven Court Records for 1644 mention "bringing bricks from the brickills in the plains"; and those for 1651 contain the following passage: "John Benham informed the Court that when this plantation was first begun, he was by the Authority then settled here, sent forth to looke for claye to make brickes, wherein he spent as much time as was worth twenty shillings, W^ch he thinkes the towne should allow him. . . ."

Early brick were very often soft and light in color and either larger or smaller than our brick of to-day. The first brick were evidently very large; the standard size then became smaller, but was finally increased to approximately that of the modern product. Investigations show that there was considerable variation in size in different localities, even at the same time. The brick used in the underpinning of the Burrage Merriam house in Rocky Hill (*circa* 1760) measure 1¾ by 3⅜ by 7 inches. There is reason to believe that these brick were first used in an earlier building. The brick of which the Robbins house, Rocky Hill (1767), were built measure 2¼ by 4 by 8½ inches. Every fourth course of the brickwork of this house is made up of alternate "headers and stretchers." The brick

"White Farm"—Long Hill

Hale House—South Coventry

Lee House—East Lyme

Peck House—Lyme

Plate XIV.

of which the old mill house or "Elm Fort" at Suffield are built measure 2 by 4 by 8 inches. Every sixth course is made up of headers, of which every alternate brick is a black or semi-vitrified brick from the arch of the kiln.

(Figure 83.) Brick used for filling between the studs of the exterior walls of the Isaac North house, Berlin (*circa* 1735), are 2½ by 4¼ by 8½ inches in size. They are laid on edge, in clay mortar. Brick which were similarly used in the Deacon Tuttle house, in West Hartford (*circa* 1700), measure 2⅜ by 4¼ by 8⅜ inches. (Figure 84.) The dimensions of a brick from the Moulthrop house in East Haven (*circa* 1690) are 1⅝ by 2⅞ by 6½ inches. Brick used in the construction of the Samuel Webster house in East Windsor Hill (1787) are of two sizes, one 2 by 3⅞ by 7¾ inches, the other 2½ by 4⅜ by 10½ inches.

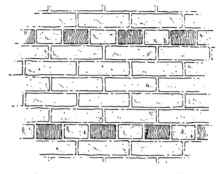

· BOND IN BRICK WALL ·
"ELM FORT"- SUFFIELD

FIGURE 83.

Brick houses were rarely built before 1750; but about that time they appear to have become popular in localities where brick were abundant. The brickwork of these houses is very often found to be of "Flemish bond"—that is, alternate headers and stretchers, the headers being of black brick, burned in the hottest part of the kiln. Such houses usually have a roof of the gambrel type; and a common feature was the insertion of the date of the building, in dark header brick, in one of the gable ends. The Joel Bradley house in North Haven (1759) is a good example. (Plate I.)

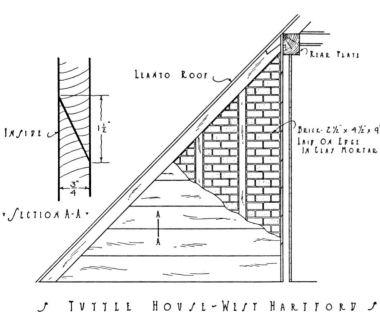

· TUTTLE HOUSE - WEST HARTFORD ·

FIGURE 84.

Another noteworthy feature in connection with brickwork is the use of a moulded course of brick in order to give a pleasing line to the offset of four inches which usually occurred between the underpinning and the walls of the first story. (Figure 85.) Brick of this sort are to be seen in the base course of the building known as "Old South Middle," on the Yale Campus in New Haven. The contour of such brick, which were especially moulded for this purpose, is a reverse curve, very pleasing.

In some houses of frame construction the practice was resorted to, as I have already mentioned in passing, of filling the spaces between the studs of the outside walls with brick, for the purpose of warmth and protection. When the Orton house in Farmington, built about 1698, was demolished recently, it was found that all the exterior walls were

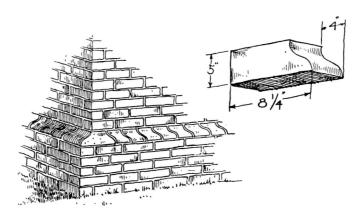

FIGURE 85.

brick-filled. The brick, however, were merely made of sun-dried clay, and were so soft that they could be broken in one's hands. They were, of course, protected from the weather by the outside covering of clapboards. The spaces between the studs of the exterior walls of the Isaac North house near Berlin (*circa* 1735) are solidly filled with brick, which were laid in clay mortar. These brick are not sun-baked, but kiln-fired. Instead of brick used in this fashion, some very old houses have exterior walls which are filled with clay between the studs. The Lyons house, on the Post Road near Greenwich (*circa* 1670), is an example. (Plate II.) There is also a tradition concerning the use of eel-grass filling in the outside walls of framed houses to secure greater warmth, but it is doubtful if this practice was ever employed to any great extent in Connecticut.

ALLYN HOUSE—WINDSOR

HYLAND-WILDMAN HOUSE—GUILFORD

WARNER HOUSE—CHESTER

CHIMNEY OF A COLLAPSED HOUSE—
CHESHIRE

PLATE XV.

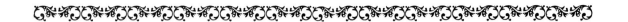

Chapter VIII. The Outside Covering

THE construction of the very earliest houses of Connecticut has already been touched upon in a previous chapter, and the possible existence considered of half-timbered work similar to that in England. There is every reason, and some documentary evidence as well, for believing that this type of construction was employed to some degree in the earliest attempts at building. The half-timbered work of England, consisting of a filling of "cob," a mixture of clay and chopped straw, between the timbers of the exterior framework, might endure in England for years, comparatively unharmed by the gently falling rains of that country. It was protected, moreover, by the widely projecting eaves of the thatch roofs. But it is obvious that exterior walls of such composition were not well suited to endure for long the rigors of an American climate. If it were successfully to withstand the driving storms of American shores, a protection of some sort over the exterior framework was indispensable.

The earliest form of such covering of which we have evidence or find any record is to be seen in the split oak clapboards which still exist in place on some of the oldest houses. In many houses of the added lean-to type, an inspection of the lean-to attic reveals, still in place, the old oak clapboards which originally covered the rear wall of the main house.

Such clapboards were "riven" or split from short oak logs, usually from four to six feet in length, by means of a special tool called a froe. This tool was very much like a knife, with a heavy broad blade about fifteen inches long, except that the handle, which was of wood, was offset and turned up at right angles to the blade. In making clapboards, a log was stood on end and split in half with this tool. Each half was again split into halves, and then into quarters, eighths, and so on, until a number of thin pieces had been produced. Owing to the radial plan of splitting, each piece was wedge-shaped in section: that is, one edge of the clapboards came to a thin or "feather" edge, while the other, or butt side, was from three-eighths to a half inch in thickness. It is evident that, because of this manner of splitting each section through the center of the log, the cleavage was in the plane of the medullary rays; so that each clapboard exhibited the markings characteristic of what is known to-day as "quartered oak."

Such clapboards of riven oak were, almost without exception, nailed directly to the studs, and the ends, which necessarily met upon a vertical stud, were bevelled and lapped in order to make the joint more nearly weatherproof. (Figure 86.)

The New Haven Court Records for June 11, 1640, mention clapboards in lengths of four, five, and six feet. Their market value was fixed as follows: "Hewing and nailing them (clapboards) on the roofes and sides of houses, well done not worth above 5s. P hundred, butt as most are done, not worth above 2s 6d." From this it is evident that the use of clapboards was not at first limited, as later, to the walls alone.

In width the early oak clapboards varied considerably, different specimens measuring from 4¾ to 8½ inches. The commonest width appears to have been about five inches, and the "weather," or exposed surface, about four inches; so that the lap was about an inch. Wider specimens were of course laid with a greater exposure to the weather.

The word "clapboard" is a provincial English term, derived from the Low German "*Klappholt*" (*Klappen* = clap, and *Holt* = wood). It originally referred, in sixteenth- and seventeenth-century English, to an oak stave used in cooperage. "Clapboards," or bolts of oak, were at that time imported to England from Germany, to be manufactured into barrel staves. They were also used to some extent for wainscoting. The German source of this material accounts for the derivation of the name.

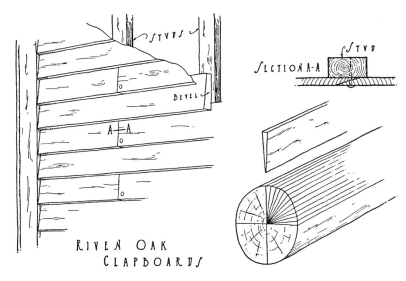

FIGURE 86.

It is probable that the colonists, finding an abundance of oak at their disposal, set about the manufacture of "clapboards" for cask staves for export to England or the West Indies. In fact, early New Haven documents mention "pipe staves, clapboards and tar" as being the first articles of export from that colony. This traffic evidently soon gave rise to fear that it might cause a shortage of lumber, for the New Haven Court Records for 1640 make mention of a fine imposed for "selling clapboards"; and in the following year, 1641, a law was passed limiting the dimensions of pipe staves.

It was apparently a short and easy step to modify these "clapboards" or pipe staves into the form which the word implies to-day, for use as a covering over the exterior house framework. A form of clapboard may be found in England on old work, but it is very doubtful if its use in Connecticut was at all traditional.

A somewhat later form of oak clapboard than the riven sort is shown in Figure 87.

FAIRCHILD HOUSE—STRATFORD

HURD HOUSE—MOODUS

KNAPP HOUSE—FAIRFIELD

BISHOP HOUSE—GUILFORD

PLATE XVI.

Clapboards of this variety were more regular in form, for instead of being split they were sawn out and in addition planed on the outside, the lower edge being finished with a one-half- or five-eighths-inch bead. Like riven clapboards, they were applied directly to the studs, and the butts lapped. Similar clapboards, said to be the original covering, are still in place on the exterior walls of the Thomas Buckingham house in Milford, for which the date of 1639 is claimed.

There are also to be found in certain regions, as a covering of very old houses, broad boards of white pine, three-fourths or seven-eighths of an inch in thickness, applied directly to the studs. The horizontal edges of such boarding have bevelled joints, so that the outside finish is flush. (Figure 88.) The Hurd house, in Moodus (1760) (Plate XVI), is completely covered with boarding of this variety. In the lean-to attic of the Loomis house in Windsor (1688), bevel-edged boards of width varying from 12 to 15 inches may still be seen covering the rear wall of the original main house.

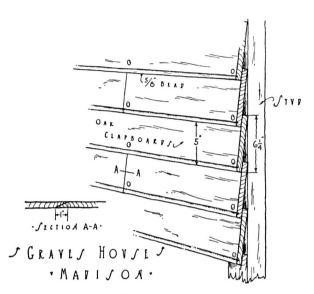

FIGURE 87.

A far commoner form of outside covering, not peculiar to any particular period, is that generally known as "weather-boarding." From Figure 89 it will be seen that weather boarding consisted of wide boards of white pine, usually about a foot in width and seven-eighths of an inch in thickness, applied to the studs in horizontal courses. The lower edge of each course, which in late work was beaded, was set into a rabbet cut in the upper edge of the course below it. "Weather boarding," as the old records have it, was sawn out, and its exposed surface planed as well. It was never so commonly used as clapboards. It often occurs on the ends and rear walls of houses, the fronts of which were clapboarded. The Bradley-Tyler house in East Haven (*circa* 1745) and the Tyler-Palmer house in Branford (*circa* 1710) are examples of this treatment. In general, weather-boarding is characteristic of late work. In such

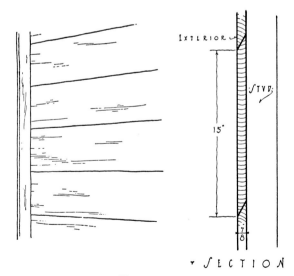

FIGURE 88.

work it was often applied in graduated courses, the lowest course being the widest, and each one above it decreasing slightly in width or "weather."

During the first quarter of the eighteenth century the use of white pine superseded that of oak as a material for outside covering; and it is doubtful if the use of riven oak clapboards continued after that time. White pine, where exposed to the weather, was more durable than oak; and this fact, together with its better working qualities, commended it to the early builders. They did not restrict themselves to the use of white pine, however, for clapboards have been found which were made of white cedar, whitewood, and hard pine or tamarack.

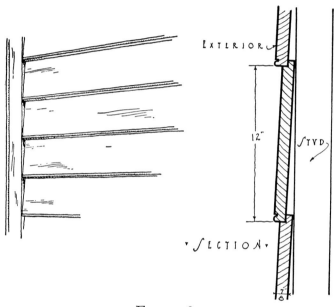

FIGURE 89.

About the middle of the eighteenth century the custom of graduating clapboards, or varying their exposure, came into vogue. Narrow clapboards were used at the sill, increasing slightly in width with successive courses; or, more often, the exposure was simply varied, the clapboards all being of the same width. Thus we find, on the front of the Samuel Mather house in Old Lyme (*circa* 1770), clapboards laid with an exposure of 1⅞ inches at the level of the sills, with a slight increase in each course above, so that at a height of ten feet above grade, the weather measures 2¼ inches. The maximum exposure is of course just below the cornice, where it measures 3½ inches. The old custom of lapping the ends of the clapboards with a bevelled joint persisted until this time; for it is a feature which almost invariably accompanies this system of graduation.

The object of the graduation, inasmuch as it was mainly confined to the fronts of houses and is rarely to be found on the sides and never on the rear, was obviously decorative. It is true, of course, that narrow exposure nearest grade meant a wider lapping of unexposed surfaces, and consequently greater warmth and security from driving storms; but had this been the main object, the practice would have been continued on all four sides of the house, as it never was.

The use of shingles as a wall covering of early houses is unusual, except in the towns of Milford, Stratford, and the surrounding locality, where it appears to have been the rule. The shingles used in this region, made of white pine, were of great length; specimens still in place measure three feet and over. In breadth they vary from 6 to 10 inches, and

PARDEE HOUSE—MONTOWESE

MORRIS HOUSE—NEW HAVEN

BRADLEY HOUSE—NEW HAVEN

KNELL HOUSE—STRATFORD

PLATE XVII.

the butts are from one-half to three-fourths of an inch in thickness. The exposure or "weather" varies, but is in the general neighborhood of eight or ten inches. The shingles which cover the Mallet house in Stratford (*circa* 1690) are laid with an exposure of fourteen inches; those on the Shelton house in the same town (1760) show an exposure of nine inches. The exterior walls of the Lyon house on the Boston Post Road, near Greenwich (*circa* 1670), are covered with hand-shaved shingles of white pine, laid with an exposure of about sixteen inches to the weather. (Plate II.) These shingles, which are claimed to be the original ones, are of uniform width, and cut in semicircular form at the butt end. Like those of the Mallett and the Shelton houses, they are secured with hand-wrought nails. In every case such shingles were cut out by hand, probably having been roughly split out at first, and then more carefully finished with a draw-shave. The durability of these shingles, used on vertical surfaces, is astonishing. Those covering the Knell house in Milford, built in 1664, are said to be the ones originally applied when the house was constructed. They are still in good condition, considering the weather they have endured with no other protection than an occasional coat of whitewash. (Plate XVII.)

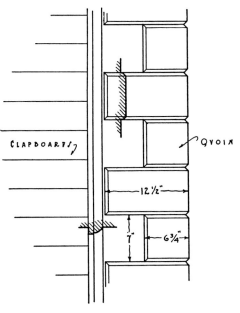

ʃ ꓲ Ꜳ O Ħ O V ʃ Ɛ - ʃ ꓲ Ꜳ ʃ B V Ʀ Y ʃ

Figure 90.

The New Haven Court Records for June 11, 1640, fixed the following prices for shingles: "Good stuff, ¾ of an inch, and 6, 7, or 8 inches broad, sorted in the woods, being 3 foote 3s 2d P hundred. 2 foote 2s. 14 inches 1s P hundred." According to Thorpe (*History of North Haven*), oak, chestnut, and cedar were all used for the manufacture of shingles, as stated in the old records. He also states that when the original shingles were removed from the roof of the Joel Bradley house in that town (1759) some years ago, they were found to be of split oak, finished on one side with a draw-shave.

The rear walls of very late houses, built about 1800 or after, were often covered, especially beneath porches, with seven-eighths-inch white pine boards, tongued and grooved, and generally beaded at the joints. Such boards were applied directly to the studs. Often they were of great width. Some on the rear wall of the Hale house in Glastonbury (*circa* 1770) measure twenty-eight inches. These boards were always horizontally applied; but the joints were not always level, because of the unequal widths of boards at opposite ends. Usually the joints run level, however, though the different courses may vary in breadth.

In certain regions, especially in and about New Haven, occasional houses built between 1800 and the beginning of the Greek Revival period have clapboarded sides and rear, and fronts covered with matched white pine boards from six to eight inches in width, horizontally applied. Two New Haven houses, the Beers house (1815) (Plate XVIII) and the Bradley house (*circa* 1820), are good examples of this treatment. The arrangement, though in itself bald, emphasizes to great advantage the fine detail about doors and windows, such as is characteristic of that period. But it was the builder's idea to give the appearance of masonry to a wooden design; and this falseness or insincerity of construction marks the beginning of the decadent period. In a way the arrangement was nevertheless an effective one. It has its exact counterpart in the "Plateresque" work of Spain, where exterior walls were kept absolutely plain, and an abundance of richly wrought detail was lavished about door and window openings.

BEERS HOUSE—NEW HAVEN

RANKIN HOUSE—GLASTONBURY

STANTON HOUSE—CLINTON

HAYDEN HOUSE—ESSEX

PLATE XVIII.

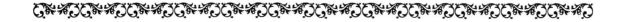

Chapter IX. Windows

IN the earliest houses built in Connecticut, what windows were considered necessary for the admittance of light and air were few and small, and that for several reasons. First, houses were the only havens of refuge in time of sudden Indian attacks, and small window openings made houses more secure. Glass was a rare and expensive article, difficult to get and hard to replace. As the available quantity was limited, this fact also had its influence in determining the size of early windows. Oiled paper and cloth were probably used to some extent, but only for a brief period and in the smaller houses.

There is but little doubt that the earliest windows were of the casement type. The New Haven Court Records for November 14, 1651, contain the following: "It is desired that the casements of the Meeting-house may haue the glass taken out and boards fitted in, that in ye winter it may bee warm; and in the summer they may bee taken down to let in ye ayre: and Jeremiah (Whitnell) was desired speedily to doe it."

Two seventeenth-century window frames, *in situ*, enable

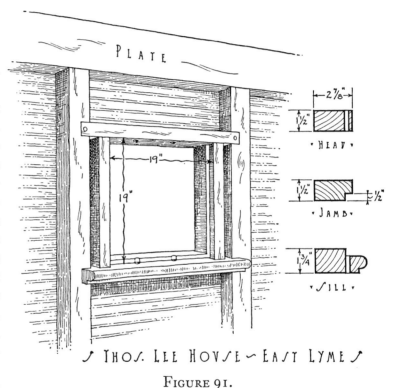

FIGURE 91.

us to get a good idea of the general type of window in use prior to 1700. One of them may be seen in the lean-to attic of the Thomas Lee house in East Lyme (1664), in what at present appears to be the rear wall of the original house. But this house, as first built, faced opposite to its present direction—the orientation of the house was changed when the lean-to was added—so that this window frame is really in the front wall of the original house. It is in the second story, just below the plate. (Figure 91.) The frame, from which the casement sash is missing, is entirely of oak. The vertical jambs on either side are tenoned into the head and sill respectively. The frame is secured in place in the customary manner, by mortising the projecting ends of the head and sill into the studs on either side. A rabbet on the outside of the frame, one-half of an inch in width, indicates the presence of sash originally. This rabbet, however, is to be found only on the sills and jambs, the head being plain. The interior edge of the frame is slightly moulded. The sash opening is small, measuring nineteen inches in each dimension; and the sill is four feet above the present floor. The purpose of the four holes, two of which are in the head and two in the sill, is uncertain. This window frame is an extremely rare specimen, and the oldest which has so far been discovered in the state.

The second example is somewhat similar. It is to be seen in the rear of the original house wall, in the attic of the added lean-to of the Shelley house in the town of Madison. The date of building of this house is uncertain; but it probably antedates 1700. The general construction of this frame, as may be seen from Figure 92, is the same as that in the Thomas Lee house. The section of the jamb, head, and sill, however, are somewhat differ-

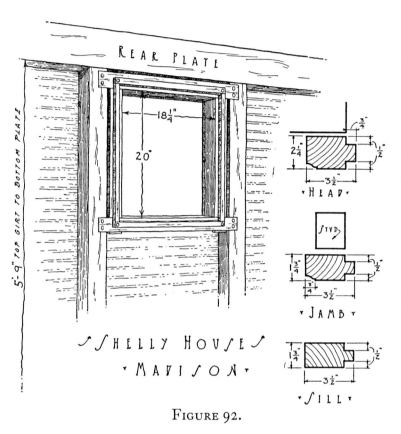

FIGURE 92.

ent. A rabbet one-half of an inch wide on the outside of the frame shows that a casement sash originally filled the opening, which is 18¼ inches wide by 20 inches in height. The frame, as may be seen, is set snugly beneath the rear plate.

A typical example of casement sash, such as was probably used in both of the window frames under discussion, is shown in Figure 93. It is at present in the Hyland-Wildman house in Guilford. From the illustration it may be seen that this sash is very thin—only three-fourths of an inch in thickness. The glazing is typical of the period, being composed of diamond-shaped lights or "quarrels," the long axes of which are set vertically. They are held together by lead bars or "calmes," slightly oval in section. The glass is extremely thin, being but one-sixteenth of an inch thick.

Assuming, as is reasonable, that the foregoing examples of early frames and sash are typical, we may safely draw the conclusion that the earliest form of window was very small, and of the casement type. Lambert, in writing of the earliest houses in his *History of New Haven Colony*, says, "The windows were of small diamond glass set in lead frames, and swung open each way on the outside." The illustrations in Lambert of Eaton's New Haven house, Governor Treat's house at Milford, and the Governor Leete house

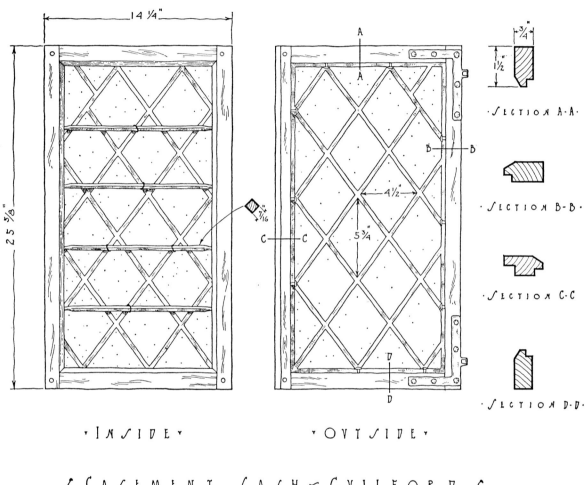

·INSIDE·   ·OUTSIDE·

CASEMENT SASH — GUILFORD

FIGURE 93.

at Guilford all show pairs of casement sash set with diamond-shaped panes. The use of casement windows probably continued for some years after 1700, for double-hung sash were not employed before the first quarter of the eighteenth century, and it is doubtful if any extended use of them was made much before 1725.

In the hall chamber of the Whitman house in Farmington (1664), marks in the wainscot indicated the presence at one time of what must have been a broad low window placed high up above the floor. If a window did originally occupy this space, its width would have been too great for a single sash, and it must therefore have been of the mullion type. It is not improbable that mullioned window frames were used before 1700; English tradition alone would suggest this.

The presence at one time of a casement window frame of mullioned form is strongly suggested by evidence found in the west gable framing of the Hempstead house in New London (1643). (Figure 69.) Two vertical studs still contain, in mortises cut into them, the broken-off tenoned ends of what was undoubtedly an earlier window frame. The vertical distance between these tenons is 21½ inches, and the space between the studs is forty-seven inches wide. Assuming the existence of a single central mullion, and allowing seven inches for its width, including that of the two jambs, we should have space for two casement sash, each 21½ inches high by about 20 inches wide— approximately the size of those in the Lee and Shelley houses.

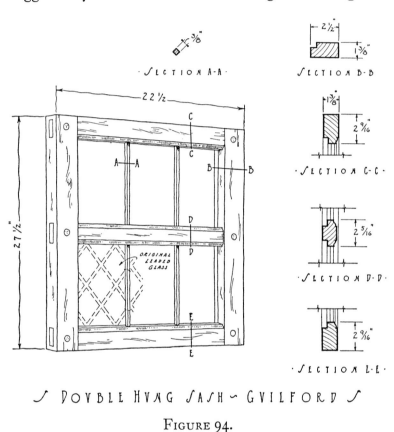

· SECTION A-A ·

· SECTION B-B ·

· SECTION C-C ·

· SECTION D-D ·

· SECTION E-E ·

ORIGINAL LEADED GLASS

∫ DOVBLE HVNG ∫A∫H ~ GVILFORD ∫

FIGURE 94.

Aside from occasional examples such as have been discussed, but few windows of the earliest type remain to us; for, like many features of our oldest houses, they were supplanted by replacements of more modern design. In many instances it is definitely known that casement sash and frames which were part of the original construction were removed, and double-hung sash and frames substituted.

A very early form of double-hung sash is illustrated in Figure 94. This sash, which is constructed of oak, was found stored in the attic of the Robinson house in Guilford, and is now in the Whitfield House Museum there. While it contains no glass, traces of leading which still adhere to the wood indicate very clearly that at one time this sash was filled with leaded glass. The panes were probably of diamond shape, similar to those in the sash illustrated in Figure 93. The glass was stiffened or supported by the horizontal wooden stays to which the leading was wired at intervals. This rare specimen is of great

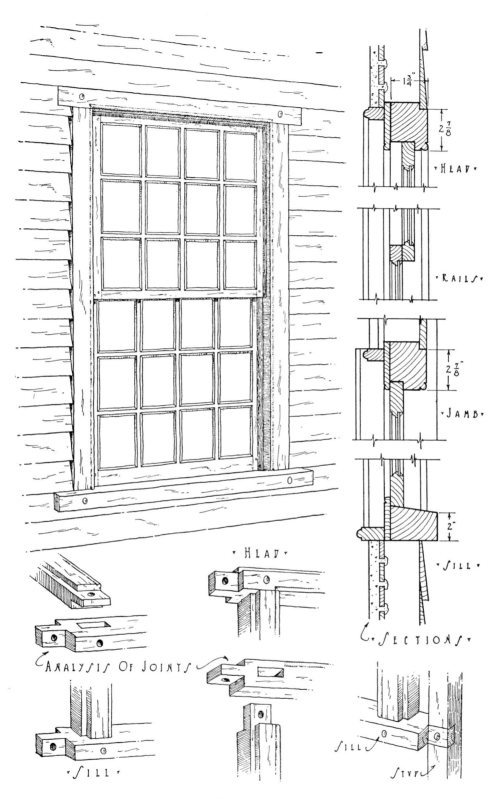

FIGURE 95.

interest due to the fact that it is a transition type, and though of double-hung form, still retains some characteristics of casement sash.

When, in the course of developments, windows of the double-hung variety having rectangular panes of glass took the place of the earlier casement type, it appears from existing examples that there was but little experimenting as to size and general proportion, for these two points soon became fixed. A pane of glass six inches wide and eight inches high was the unit which determined both the size of the sash and the proportion of the window frame. The earlier forms of double-hung sash, almost without exception, are composed of these 6-by-8-inch lights, which were evidently a standard size. Sash which were four lights wide were quite invariably the rule, though in height they varied, being two, three, and four lights high. The earliest type of double-hung window with rectangular panes is that whose lower sash is two lights high and the upper three, or *vice versa*. A later and more common arrangement consists of a window containing two sash of equal height, each containing twelve 6-by-8-inch lights, as in Figure 95. With the adoption of the 6-by-8-inch light as a standard, there came another change which should not be overlooked. Sash were no longer constructed of oak, but of white pine instead.

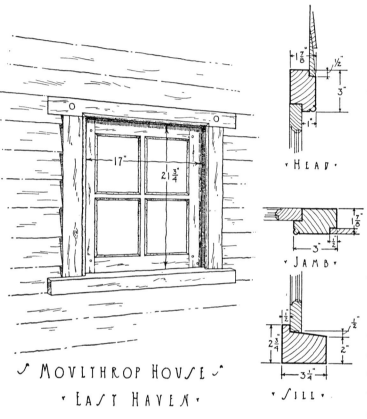

· HEAD ·

· JAMB ·

· SILL ·

✒ MOULTHROP HOUSE ✒

· EAST HAVEN ·

FIGURE 96.

In windows of the double-hung type, the upper sash was fixed, being rabbeted into the frame. The lower sash only was operated; it slid up and down and was held at various heights by a spring catch on the jamb. The counterbalanced sash of modern type, with its pockets in the jambs for weights, was as yet unthought of. The frames of these early windows were of solid oak construction, similar to those of the casement variety. The jambs were framed into the head and sill by means of the customary tusk-tenon-and-mortise joint, and secured in place by wooden pins. Like its predecessor of the casement type, the window frame was secured in place by mortising the projecting ends of the head and sill into the studs on either side. The construction of a typical window of this type is shown in Figure 95.

WARNER HOUSE—CHESTER

PITKIN HOUSE—EAST HARTFORD

WELLES-SHIPMAN HOUSE—
SOUTH GLASTONBURY

WHEELER-BEECHER HOUSE—BETHANY

PLATE XIX.

Since walls were generally constructed of 3-by-4-inch studs set flatwise, with less than one inch of lath and plaster on the inside and clapboards nailed directly to them on the exterior, the total thickness of outside walls was in the neighborhood of five inches. If the house were of "plank-frame" construction, this was still less. Window trim was at first set flush with the plaster on the inside, so that the two sash, each an inch thick, brought the outside of the window frame, with its enclosing rabbet, out beyond the face of the exterior wall covering. This is a marked characteristic of these early window frames. Another feature common to them is the projection of the head and sill beyond each side of the jambs, as shown in Figures 95 and 96.

One of the first attempts to elaborate the double-hung window frame on the exterior was the addition of a cornice or pediment to its head. This form of ornamentation often accompanies the heavy projecting frame previously described. The windows on the front of the Belden house in Wethersfield (*circa* 1753) and of the Trumbull house in North Haven (1761) are examples of such treatment. (Figure 97.) From the drawing of the Belden house windows it will be seen that there is a slight break of offset in the rake mouldings, just above their

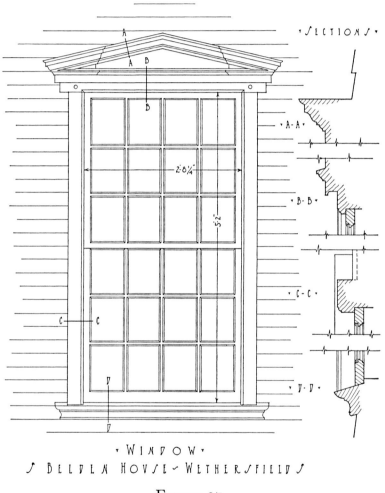

· W I N D O W ·

ſ B E L D E N H O V ſ E ~ W E T H E R ſ F I E L D ſ

FIGURE 97.

intersection with the horizontal members. This is a characteristic feature of these pedimented window heads, which are common to the period 1740-1750. They appear to belong chiefly to houses of the central-chimney type. Very often this form of elaboration is to be found only on the front of the house, the windows on the ends and rear being quite plain.

In the general process of refinement which was continually at work, and which was recorded in every part of the house fabric, the exterior window treatment was naturally affected, and underwent certain changes. Especially with the abandonment of plank-frame construction and the adoption of sheathing over the exterior framework, an important change was wrought. Thanks to the resulting increase in the thickness of walls, which was further augmented by setting the interior trim out beyond the surface of the plaster, the sash were no longer set so far forward, and the frame itself was covered by an outside casing. This exterior casing, which in turn came to be finished with one or more mouldings, thus took on the character of an architrave. About 1800, or later, a frieze was added to the top of the window above the architrave, and the whole surmounted with a cornice. (Figure 98.) Sometimes the frieze was carved with groups of short vertical flutes or otherwise ornamented, and the cornice enriched by the introduction of dentils and delicate modillion brackets. An example from a house in New Haven, built about 1800, has dainty modillions of this sort which measure but one inch in width and 1¾ inches in their projection.

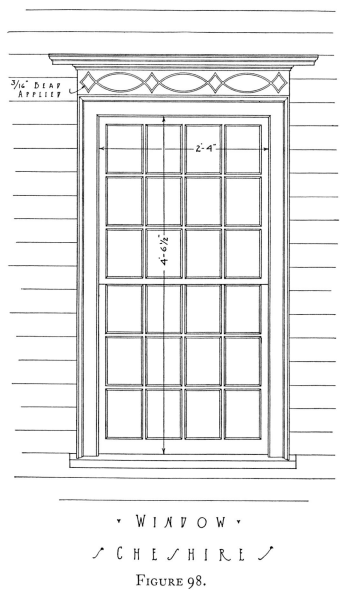

• W I N D O W •

╱ C H E S H I R E ╱

FIGURE 98.

Curiously, the sills, which in earlier work had been handsomely moulded, as in Figure 97, generally became quite plain after the adoption of the outside casing, or architrave.

Sash, up till a very late period, were constructed from "inch stock," the average thickness being but seven-eighths of an inch. After 1800 sash increased in thickness to 1⅜ inches. White pine, because of its durability and the ease of working it, was the material invariably used for sash. The corners of the sash were mortised and tenoned together and secured by wooden pins, according to modern practice. Rails were narrow, and the meeting rails still smaller, rarely being more than an inch wide. The bottom rail, which meets the sill, was very seldom more than two inches in height.

Sash bars, or muntins, in early work measure as much as 1¼ inches in width (Figure 99), the average up to about the last quarter of the eighteenth century being about one inch. About that time a decided narrowing took place, until, in work executed after 1800, the muntin is extremely thin and characterless. This change was largely due, no doubt, to the increased thickness of the sash material; the muntin became correspondingly thin and deep in section, rather than broad and shallow. The same muntin section was used repeatedly in early sash, and there was practically no variation from the one type. (Figure 99.)

· OVT/IDE ·

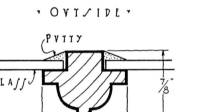

FIGURE 99.

Because the muntins of these early sash were broad and flat, and the panes of glass small, the sash area was covered by a lattice-like arrangement of wooden sash bars which carried across the window openings some of the feeling of solidity properly belonging to the outside walls of the house. It is apparent, then, that windows fitted with such sash hardly played the part of voids in the design of the house exterior. This impression was still further heightened by the way the sash were set in their frames. They were placed well forward— almost on the same vertical plane as that of the outside wall. Accordingly, but little shadow was cast by the heads and jambs of the window frames upon the sash. These two

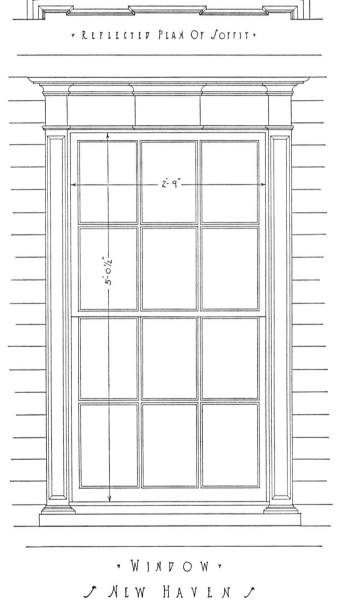

· REFLECTED PLAN OF SOFFIT ·

· WINDOW ·
/ NEW HAVEN /

FIGURE 100.

reasons—the flatness and width of the muntins, and the lack of shadows at the window openings—account largely for the bluff, almost bald appearance which is so characteristic of many of the early houses.

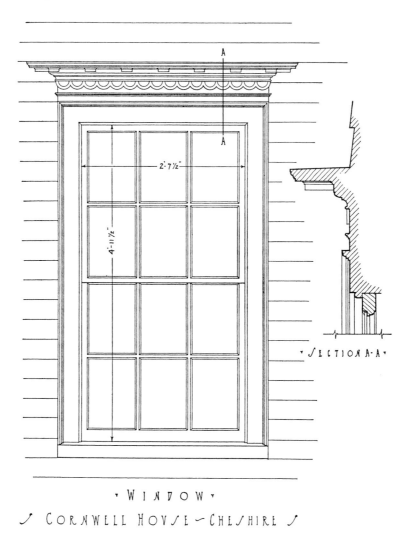

· W I N D O W ·

ᶴ C O R N W E L L H O V ᶴ E — C H E ᶴ H I R E ᶴ

FIGURE 101.

Not until the muntin section became narrower and deeper did the custom abate of setting the glass very close to the outer surface of the sash. Eventually glass increased in size, and the dimensions of the individual pane became 8 by 12 inches. Six lights thereupon replaced the earlier arrangement of twelve. It should be noted that, although the panes became larger, the dimensions of the sash remained as formerly. (Figure 100.)

The first glass used was brought from England, which continued to be the source of supply for a considerable period. There were early attempts at glass making in the Colonies,

BROOKS HOUSE—STRATFORD

MacCURDY HOUSE—LYME

DEMING HOUSE—WETHERSFIELD

WARHAM WILLIAMS HOUSE—NORTHFORD

PLATE XX.

but they proved unsuccessful. The low rates of carriage on boxed glass from England undoubtedly had much to do with the continued use of that product. Boxed glass, which is both compact and heavy, may early have served as ballast.

Although the manufacture of glass is as ancient as history, it was not until the seventeenth century that a patent was granted for its fabrication in England. William Penn, in a letter written in 1638, referred to an unsuccessful attempt to establish a "glass-house" in America. The venture of eccentric Baron Steigel at Mannheim, Pa., was likewise a failure. In 1747 Thomas Darling of New Haven was granted an exclusive right by the court to make glass during a period of twenty years. It was stipulated, however, that he

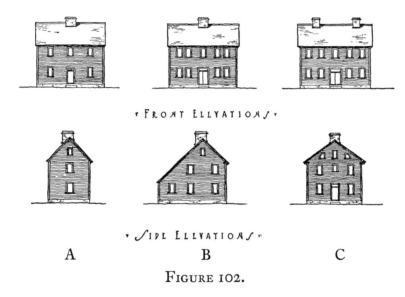

· FRONT ELEVATIONS ·

· SIDE ELEVATIONS ·

A   B   C

FIGURE 102.

should make five hundred feet in four years! Even during the Revolutionary period glass was scarce, and that made in America was of poor quality. Its manufacture was not established on a commercial basis until 1792.

English glass was made up of four or five different grades, the best of which was "Crown glass." "Newcastle glass" was next in quality; this was the sort commonly used for window glazing. "Phial glass" was of poor quality, greenish in color and streaked with air bubbles.

It is always easy to distinguish old glass, because of its uneven surface and its amber or violet hue, due to the presence of manganese. Another common characteristic of old glass is its metallic iridescence.

Very often a valuable clue to the period to which a house belongs can be obtained through a study of its fenestration. This is especially true of the window arrangement or grouping of the front elevation. In Connecticut there appear to be three general methods of composition. (Figure 102.) First, there is that in which the facade has five window openings—one in the center of the wall of each front room, and one above the front entrance, as in A. This arrangement is typical of the central-chimney house of two-room plan. This was followed by the introduction of an additional window for each front room, making nine on

HUMISTON HOUSE—HAMDEN

WELLES-SHIPMAN HOUSE—
SOUTH GLASTONBURY

OLD TAVERN—ROCKY HILL

ENTRANCE OF AN OLD HOUSE—WINDSOR

PLATE XXII.

The front door of the William Judson house in Stratford (1723) contains four such lights, arranged in a row, and separated by heavy moulded muntins. Each pane measures 7¼ inches wide by 9½ inches high, and is about one inch thick at the center. The use of glass in the door itself, after this fashion, is decidedly unusual. (Figure 109.)

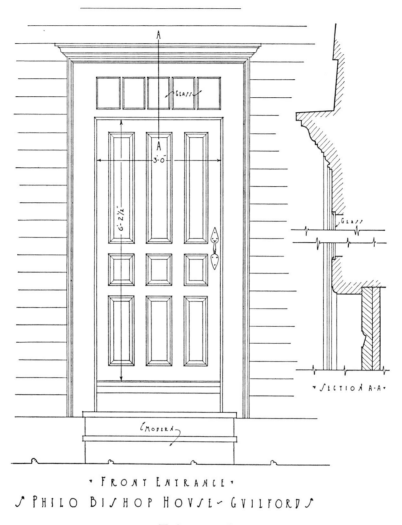

· FRONT ENTRANCE ·
ᶴ PHILO BISHOP HOUSE ~ GUILFORD ᶴ

FIGURE 108.

The "Dutch" or, as it is sometimes called, "hatchet" door is probably of early appearance. (Figure 107.) Although its use persisted until a late date, it is not of common occurrence. The panelled door made its appearance about 1700. At first it was of simple form, with rectangular panels. These gradually increased in number and became of elaborate form. Panelled doors were commonly reinforced on the back, or inner side, with a three-fourths or one-inch sheathing, applied with horizontal joints. Even when this arrangement exists, the total thickness of the door is not more than two inches. The single door, at first

GLASS

3'-2½"

6'-7½"

· FRONT ENTRANCE ·

ʃ Wᴹ· JVDSON HOVSE - STRATFORD ʃ

FIGURE 109.

comparatively narrow, gradually became wider, and was eventually replaced by a pair of doors. Single doors were rarely wider than three feet, although the original front door of the Commodore Hull house in Shelton (1771), which is of the "Dutch" type, measures 3 feet 4 inches in width. Double or two-leaf doors were nearly always each two feet in width, so that the total width of the door opening is always close to four feet. The average door height is 6 feet 8 or 10 inches; and it rarely exceeds seven feet.

· FRONT ·   · SIDE ·

· FRONT ENTRANCE ·

⸭ TYLER HOUSE ~ BRANFORD ⸭

FIGURE 110.

The hooded entrance, such as that of the Tyler house in Branford (*circa* 1710) is of rare form. (Figure 110.) It is strongly suggestive of Dutch influence, traces of which occasionally occur, and which probably found its way into Connecticut *via* Long Island or up the Sound.

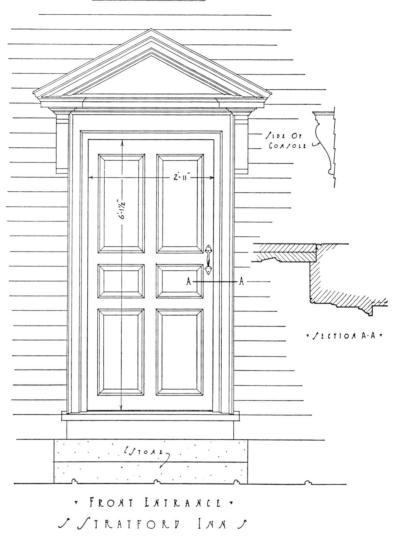

· FRONT ENTRANCE ·
S STRATFORD INN S

FIGURE 111.

Entrances similar to that of the old Stratford Inn, built about 1745, and now demolished, which consist of a simply panelled door surmounted by a pediment carried on consoles, are not common. (Figure 111.) This type of doorway appears to belong almost exclusively to Stratford.

The next development beyond the doorway which consists of a simple moulded architrave was marked by the use of pilasters, one at either side of the entrance. When pilasters

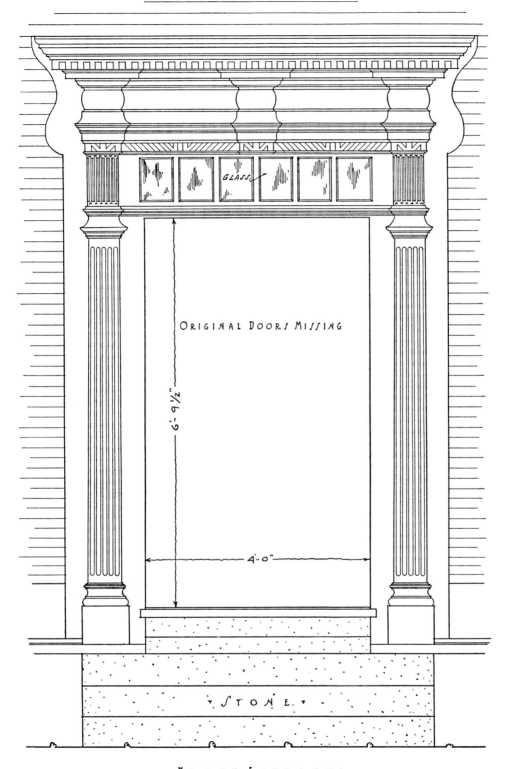

GLASS

ORIGINAL DOORS MISSING

6'-9½"

4'-0"

STONE

· FRONT ENTRANCE ·

ʃ SAMVEL MATHER HOVSE ~ LYME ʃ

FIGURE 112.

were so employed, the entablature which they supported was generally treated in one of three ways. The first and simplest was the conventional arrangement of three main horizontal divisions: namely, architrave, frieze, and cornice. In the second form, the cornice members are treated as a pediment; and in the third the pediment is broken, the cornice members assuming a reverse curve and terminating in a circular carved rosette. The last two types were much in vogue about the middle of the eighteenth century, and the glazed transom composed of small panes is never found in connection with them.

The front entrance of the Samuel Mather house in Lyme (*circa* 1770) is an excellent example of the first of these three types which we have to consider. (Figure 112.) The door opening, from which the original doors are unfortunately missing, measures four feet in width by 6 feet 9½ inches in height. Pilasters of seven-eighths-inch projection, having five shallow flutes, flank the door on either side. They have high moulded bases, made up of the steep mouldings typical of the period, supported by plinths which are nearly square. The mouldings of which the pilaster caps are composed are of similar mode, and bear no semblance of Classic forms; the Jacobean note is still predominant. Directly above the door is a moulded transom bar, the ends of which are mitered into, and form the top members of, the pilaster caps. Above the transom bar is the conventional arrangement of six lights of seven by ten inch glass. The space above the pilasters is occupied by blocks of triglyph-like form, which have five vertical channels of triangular section. They are of the same width as the pilasters, which have no entasis. The lowest member of the architrave is carved with shallow sinkages; above it, plain and moulded members alternate. The frieze, which is plain, is of pulvinated form. Mouldings of Classic form appear in the cornice, which is not, however, Classic in its composition or contour. Very characteristic are the shallow sinkages carved in the corona, forming a suggestion of dentil treatment. The breaks formed by the pilasters and the central motive are not carried above the corona member. A feature to be noted is the board which forms the clapboard stop, on the outer side of the pilasters. The portion of it which is opposite the entablature has been given a fanciful form; whereas usually it is simply splayed outward and terminates at the end of the cornice.

The front entrance of the Trumbull house in North Haven (1761) may be regarded as not only a typical, but actually an excellent example of the pilastered doorway of the pedimented type. (Figure 113.) There again the original doors are missing. The opening measures 4 feet 2 inches in width by 7 feet 1½ inches in height. A pilaster without entasis, of 6¼ inches' width and ⅞ inch projection, and having five shallow flutes, is supported by a pedestal on either side of the door. The die of each pedestal is filled with a round-headed panel. The mouldings forming the pedestal cap and the pilaster base are so combined that they form one group. Here, as in the pilaster capitals, there is strong Jacobean feeling; for there is but little suggestion of the Classic in either the individual mouldings or their composition. The pilaster capitals are simple, and their tops line with the door head. The height of the necking, which is greater than the width of the pilaster, contains a six-petalled rosette in shallow carving. This form of decoration is a favorite one for this place; it recurs again and again. Strongly suggestive of the Tudor rose, it is undoubtedly

ROBINSON HOUSE—SOUTHINGTON

THOMPSON HOUSE—FARMINGTON

OLD INN—EAST WINDSOR

GRISWOLD HOUSE—GUILFORD

PLATE XXIII.

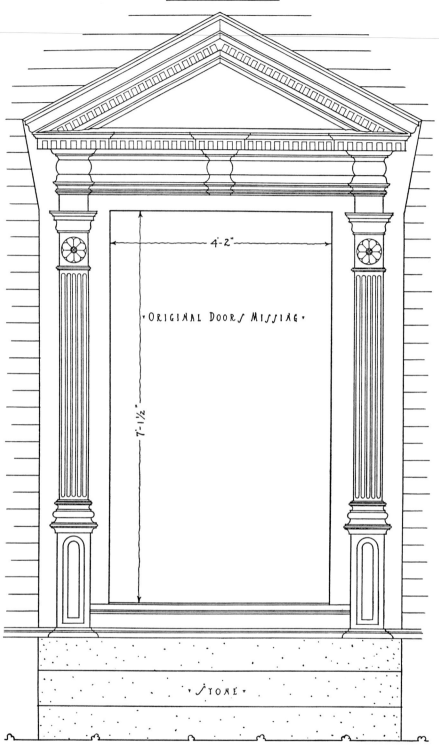

4'-2"

·ORIGINAL DOORS MISSING·

7'-1½"

·STONE·

·FRONT ENTRANCE·

♪ TRVMBVLL HOVSE~NORTH HAVEN ♪

FIGURE 113.

a recrudescence from that period. From the top of the door opening to the bottom of the architrave is a space of 4¾ inches. The architrave is composed of a group of narrow mouldings which have little relation to each other. A narrow frieze, of but 3¼ inches in height, is of the usual pulvinated form. The cornice is the only part of the entablature which shows any Classical spirit. Its corona exhibits the customary dentil-like treatment in the form of slight sinkages, carved but three-sixteenths of an inch deep. The very steep pitch of the pediment is a characteristic feature, as is also the central break in the entablature, which repeats the breaks on either side of it. As is customary, the board forming the clapboard stop on the outside of each pilaster splays outward to meet the lower angle of the pediment.

The third type of pilastered doorway, with a broken scroll pediment, is typically represented by the front entrance of the Warham Williams house in Northford (1750), shown in Figure 114. Each door is two feet wide (giving us the usual total width of four feet) by six feet seven inches in height. These doors are of double thickness, and simply panelled. Each leaf is hung on a pair of wrought-iron strap hinges placed on the inside, which reach nearly across the width of the door. Both doors are fastened by means of an oak bar which is dropped into two iron staples, driven into the jambs on the inside. This was a typical mode of door fastening. The pilaster treatment is very similar to that of the Trumbull house doorway. The pilasters project one inch, and each has five shallow flutes. The pedestals which support them have each a round-headed panel, of the usual "bead and bevel" section, in its die—a typical arrangement, as is the single group of mouldings forming the pilaster base and pedestal cap. The pilaster capitals are fairly Classical in their composition, though not in the flavor of their mouldings. The necking, which is high, contains the customary carved rosette, which in this example is of double form. The pilasters exhibit the usual lack of entasis. From the head of the door to the bottom of the architrave is a space of six inches, which is carried around the door opening and cut with shallow three-eighths-inch grooves, crudely suggestive of masonry jointing. The same treatment is repeated on the board forming the clapboard stop, on the outer side of each pilaster. This is a characteristic, in fact almost invariable, feature of this type of doorway. The entablature groups itself into three natural divisions. The architrave is made up of alternated mouldings and plain fillets; as usual, Classical feeling is entirely lacking from its composition. The narrow pulvinated frieze measures but 3½ inches in height. The cornice is of fairly regular composition, its principal member being a broad corona which does not bear the customary denticulated carving, such as is displayed by the doorway of the Old Inn at East Windsor (*circa* 1753). (Plate XXIII.) The crown moulding of the cornice rises in a steep curve of reverse form, and terminates on each side in a carved rosette of the usual six-petalled shape. Its course is repeated by the members which occur beneath it. Its abrupt rise and its general steepness of contour give the whole composition a great deal of style and distinction, utterly lacking in certain late examples, which display a flatter curve of more "lazy" outline. The central break extending up through the entablature supports a narrow panelled pedestal, the top of which is connected by loop-shaped

· STONE ·

· FRONT ENTRANCE ·

ʃ WARHAM WILLIAMʃ HOVʃE ~ NORTHFORD ʃ

FIGURE 114.

mouldings with the rosettes on each side. This pedestal, in doorways of this type, often supports some form of carved or turned ornament. The whole scroll arrangement of this entrance is flashed with heavy sheet lead, a survival of English usage.

Entrances of this type were occasionally executed in a much elaborated form, bordering on ornateness. The doorways of the Grant house in East Windsor (1757-1758) (Frontis-

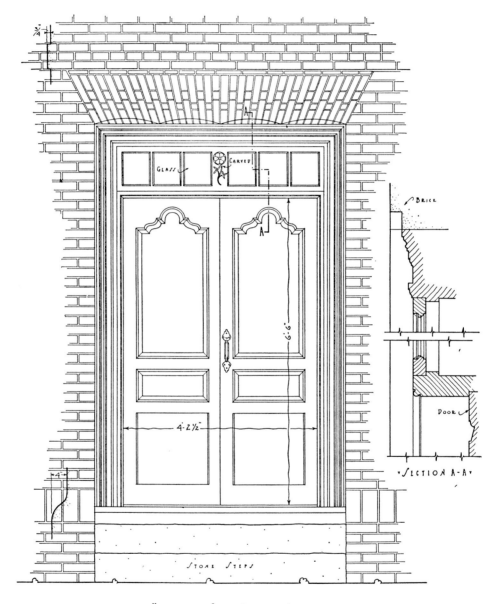

· FRONT ENTRANCE ·

· COLONEL BARKER HOUSE ~ NORTH HAVEN ·

FIGURE 115.

RANKIN HOUSE—GLASTONBURY

HILL HOUSE—GLASTONBURY

BASSETT HOUSE—HAMDEN

"THE PARSONAGE"—MONROE

PLATE **XXIV.**

piece) and of the Old Inn at the same place are examples. (Plate XXIII.) The Grant house entrance is the earlier of the two, and its feeling throughout is strongly suggestive of Jacobean work. This is especially true of many of the mouldings, which are beak-like in section. Elaborately panelled doors are characteristic of this type of doorway, diagonally crossed stiles in the lower part of the door being a favorite arrangement.

An interesting and unusual variation of this type of entrance is the doorway of the Captain Charles Churchill house, built in 1763, which once stood in the town of Newington. The whole entablature was carried out beyond the lower part of the doorway by the projecting second-story overhang, which was of the hewn type. Several feet on either side of the doorway, this overhang was framed down so that it corresponded in level with the height of the doorhead. As far as is known, this is an unique example of such treatment in Connecticut. Fortunately this fine entrance has been preserved in the Athenæum at Hartford.

These three types of entrances have been described at considerable length, because they are typical doorways of the earlier Connecticut houses, built up to 1750 or Revolutionary times. After that time, thanks to the constant search for elaboration, different types made their appearance—principally, the columnar "porch" and the elliptical-headed entrance with fan- and side-lights of leaded glass.

Chapter XI. Front Entrances: Later Types

THE columnar front entrance does not appear to be an integral part of houses built before the last quarter of the eighteenth century. It is a distinctively Georgian institution, and its prototype is to be found in English work of the period. It is, then, invariably an indication of late work. It was used principally from 1800 onward to the beginning of the Greek Revival period; and it reached its highest development and greatest elegance of proportion and of detail in the years between 1810 and 1820. It is more especially a feature of the pretentious and sophisticated city house than of its country relative; and it belongs almost exclusively to the central-hall type of plan.

In its commonest form, this type of entrance consists of a single door, above which is a semielliptical or semicircular fan-light of leaded glass, flanked on either side by pilasters, on the axes of which are columns supporting a gabled roof, the outer end of which is open. The distance between the pilasters and the columns in front of them, though variable, is generally in the neighborhood of two or three feet. The columns and the entablature above them are usually Classical in proportion and detail, though in many cases the canons of Vignola were overborne by the inventive ingenuity of the builder. It will be seen that the arrangement of a gable roof abutting the house is but a development of the pilastered entrance carrying a pediment overhead: the scheme is fundamentally the same, except that the pediment has been extended forward and its open end supported by columns.

This type of "porch" (the word is used in its modern sense) may be divided into two groups. In the first may be included all the work in which Classical precedent and proportions were followed with more or less exactitude. The second contains entrances the builders of which gave free rein to their own ingenuity, introducing new proportions in designs which were more personal and individual in expression.

As an example of the first group, we may take the entrance porch of the Bassett house in the town of Hamden, which quite closely approximates Classical lines. It is a typical Georgian porch of late date, built with the house in 1819. (Plate XXIV.) The door is a single one simply panelled. Its construction is quite different from that of doors of older type: substantial rails and stiles, 1¾ inches thick, enclose thinner panels, which are secured in place by a separate set of mouldings. The old bead-and-bevel panel section has disappeared; it is rarely, if ever, found in work of this date. Panels of curved or decorative contour have also given way to plain rectangular forms. It is of interest to note that, in general, doors have increased in height, although this particular example measures but seven feet.

The fan-light above the door, so named from its radiating lead bars, is semielliptical in shape. A moulded transom bar is mitered to form the caps of the pilasters on each side of the door, where it intersects them. The fan-light is enclosed by trim of moulded sec-

COLONEL HITCHCOCK HOUSE—CHESHIRE

ENTRANCE OF AN OLD HOUSE—
REDDING RIDGE

OLD TAVERN—STRAITSVILLE

MAJOR TALMAGE HOUSE—GUILFORD

PLATE XXV.

tion, which is divided by a moulded key block at the center of the arch. The glazing of the fan-light is held in place by lead bars, and ornamented by leaden festoons and rosettes, typical of the period. The custom of setting the glass well forward in its frame has still persisted; here we find it on the same plane as the outer surface of the frame.

The arrangement of columns and the pilasters behind them is typical. The columns, which are of the Roman Doric order, have bases and capitals of conventional Classical form; the shafts, which display an entasis, are turned from solid pieces of maple.

The entablature is of regular proportions, being composed of a moulded architrave, a plain frieze, and an elaborate cornice into which have been introduced a dentil course and delicate modillion brackets. Sawed-out modillions of fine scale almost invariably accompany this type of entrance, and a common arrangement is to be seen in the introduction of a single bracket at the very apex of the gable.

The soffit of the roof we may expect to find either panelled, as in this example, or finished with a flattened vault of plaster. The porch of the Rankin house in Glastonbury (1754), which is of later date than the house, affords us an example of the latter treatment. (Plate XXIV.)

A very pleasing feature of the example under consideration is the gentle sweep with which the rake mouldings form their lower termination. This softening of outline is repeated in the gables of the house as well.

This entrance is an admirable illustration of a subject discussed in the chapter on

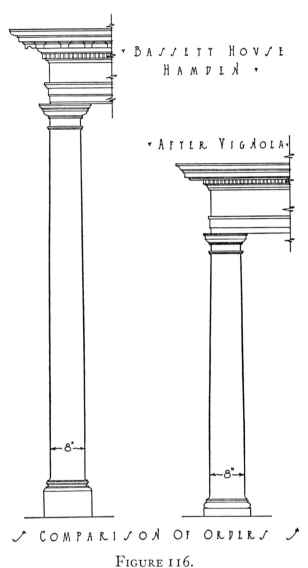

· BASSETT HOUSE HAMDEN ·

· AFTER VIGNOLA·

← 8'→

← 8"→

♪ COMPARISON OF ORDERS ♪

FIGURE 116.

Mouldings: namely, the translation which was so skillfully effected in converting the proportion of a stone idiom to one of wood. Figure 116 shows the order employed in the Bassett house entrance, drawn first according to the canons of Vignola (A) and then as it is actually executed (B). In A the diameter of the column, eight inches, is taken as the unit of measurement. It will be seen that the wooden column of new proportion is about 10½

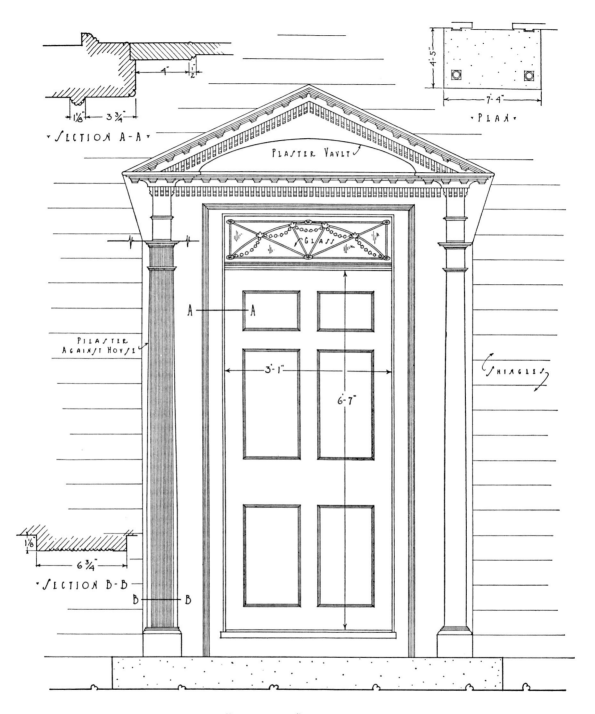

· SECTION A-A ·

4"

1/2"

1 1/8"   3 3/4"

· PLAN ·

4'-5"

7'-4"

PLASTER VAVLT

· GLASS ·

PILASTER
AGAINST HOVSE

A — A

3'-1"

6'-7"

SHINGLES

1 1/8"

6 3/4"

· SECTION B-B ·

B — B

· FRONT ENTRANCE ·
S HAWLEY HOVSE ~ MONROE S

FIGURE 117.

WHITMAN HOUSE—WEST HARTFORD

DEMING HOUSE—FARMINGTON

CHAMBERLAIN HOUSE—GUILFORD

COLONEL LEWIS HOUSE—ESSEX

PLATE XXVI.

diameters high, whereas the stone column, in accordance with Vignola's standards, is but eight diameters. This comparison is of value in that it clearly shows how an understanding of the new material, thus finally arrived at, made possible an architecture of greater lightness, grace, and elegance.

The second of our types, that in which the builder's originality was allowed freer scope and Classical lines were less closely followed, may be found embodied in the front entrance porch of the Cyrus Hawley house in Monroe (*circa* 1740). (Figure 117.)

The door, which is of six-panel form, is very similar to that of the Bassett house. The transom above it, however, is rectangular. Its glazing is of the usual sort: leaded, with applied festoons and ornaments of lead. Instead of the conventional architrave about the door opening, there is merely a simple beaded moulding, applied to the plain surface.

The original columns of this porch are, very unfortunately, missing; an attempted restoration has been made in the drawing. Possibly the supports in this case were simply chamfered posts, with moulded caps and bases. The entablature is of great interest, in that it bears no relation to its stone antecedents save in its division into three main parts. Architrave, frieze, and cornice are all represented, but not in conventional form. Behind the columns, and against the house, are placed very flat pilasters, the vertical surfaces of which are finely beaded.

Architrave and frieze, both perfectly plain, are separated only by a narrow moulding of beak-like section, but three-eighths of an inch in width. The bottom member of the cornice is formed by a course of dentils, the lower ends of which are curiously cut, applied directly to the frieze. Above this are a shallow coved moulding of wide projection and block-like brackets, each of which is made up of three members. Three simple fillets, the uppermost of which is rounded, crown the whole. Composed of but few members, and of great simplicity, this cornice is peculiarly rich in its effect. The soffit of the porch roof is a very flat vault, semielliptical in section, finished in plaster. There is little of Georgian flavor about such a composition; it smacks too strongly of the personality and inventiveness of its builder. The individual touch is unmistakable.

A point to be noted in connection with porches of the columnar type is that the earliest specimens had roofs which were of a much steeper pitch than those built during the later periods. In the examples of later date the pitch became much flattened. The Tuscan appears to have been the most popular order, judging from the frequency with which it occurs; next to it comes the Ionic, with capitals usually of the Scamozzi form. The Corinthian order, except in the very latest periods, was rarely used in Connecticut. Plain shafts are to be found much oftener than fluted ones, which divide honors about equally with those of the reeded type.

Another variation of the columnar porch has a flat roof and an entablature which is carried around horizontally. Entrance porches of this type, usually very late work, border upon the Greek Revival period. Still another type of front entrance—one which belongs almost exclusively to the central-hall house—is that which displays a central door flanked with side-lights, and a fan-light of semielliptical form surmounting the whole. Entrances

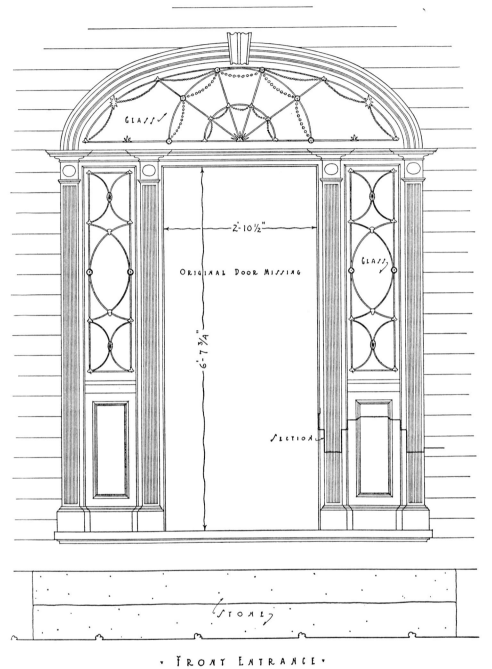

GLASS

GLASS

GLASS

2'-10½"

ORIGINAL DOOR MISSING

6'-7¾"

SECTION

STONE

· FRONT ENTRANCE ·

CORNWELL HOVSE ~ CHESHIRE

FIGURE 118.

of this sort are built into the house wall and do not project beyond it. The front entrance of the Cornwell house in Cheshire (*circa* 1820) is a typical example. (Figure 118.) The original door of this entrance is missing; but it is said to have been of the regular six-panelled type. The opening measures 3 feet 1 inch in width by 6 feet 8 inches in height. It is flanked by rectangular side-lights, 11½ inches wide, the tops of which line with that of the door opening. The sills of these side-lights are a little below the middle of the door, and the space beneath them

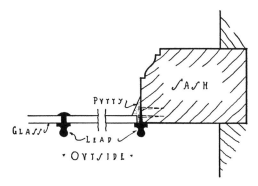

FIGURE 119.

is panelled. The door jambs, which form mullions between the door and each side-light, are treated somewhat as pilasters, the moulded transom bar being mitered to form their caps. The side-lights are filled with glass set in lead bars, the intersections of which, as in the transom, are covered with applied ornaments of cast lead. Door and side-lights are

crowned by a large transom or fan-light of semielliptical shape, glazed in the same fashion as the side-lights. A handsomely moulded key block is set into the trim which frames it. In both the fan- and side-lights the glass is set flush with the exterior surface of the sash frames. A section showing this construction is shown in Figure 119. This appears to have been the typical manner of installing leaded glass.

Ornaments of cast lead such as were used to embellish the glass of this entrance are to be found in a great variety of forms and sizes. Various fruits, such as the blackberry and the pineapple, leaves of various form, human faces, and the more conventional rosette are all commonly met with, cleverly applied as spots of decoration to cover the intersec-

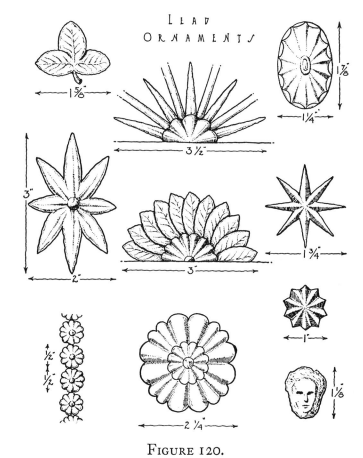

FIGURE 120.

· L E A D   O R N A M E N T ·

E L Y   H O U S E ~ E L Y'S   L A N D I N G

FIGURE 121.

tions of the calmes or lead bars. (Figure 120.) In fan-lights, the lead bars of which radiate from a common center, there was customarily placed an ornament somewhat on the order of a sunburst, such as is shown in Figure 121. The lead eagle, shown in Figure 122, measuring nine inches from tip to tip of its wings, is an unusually fine specimen of the lead-worker's art. This ornament was taken from the transom over the doorway of an old house standing on Meadow Street, New Haven.

Another type of entrance doorway which is also flush with the house wall, commonly seen in houses built during the last decade of the eighteenth century or later, is that having, on either side of the door, pilasters which carry an entablature, the cornice of which is of pedimented form and encloses a semicircular transom of leaded glass. The front entrance of the Colonel Lewis house (*circa* 1775) illustrates this type. (Plate XXVI.)

Certain large and rather pretentious houses of very late date, such as the Prudence Crandall house in Canterbury (*circa* 1815) and the Gay house in Suffield (1795), display front entrances which are part of a very elaborate motive. (Plates XXI and XXVII.) Treatment of this sort is, however, uncommon, and does not occur with sufficient frequency to mark it as a type. Nor can entrances such as those of the Sheldon Tavern in Litchfield (1795) and the Cowles house in Farmington (Plates XXVII and VI) be regarded as representing a type. These entrances, together with several others like them, are so strikingly similar in treatment as well as unusual in conception that the traditional attribution of their design to an officer of Burgoyne's army who was paroled in Connecticut during the Revolutionary war, may well be accredited.

Side entrances, which occurred in houses of the central-chimney type on the sunny or garden side of the house, near the front corner and opening directly into the hall, were usually very plain and simple. Even when the front entrance was of considerable pretensions, this "garden door" was generally nothing more than a plain panelled door, framed by a moulded architrave, and with perhaps a frieze and simple cornice. (Figure

FIGURE 122.

123.) It is in this place that the Dutch door is most commonly found; but there are never transoms or side-lights.

When the house is of the central-hall type, the side entrance is usually more elaborate. That of the Gay house in Suffield (1795) is treated with engaged columns of the Ionic order; that of the Champion house in East Haddam (1794) (Plate

DEMING HOUSE—LITCHFIELD

WHEELER-BEECHER HOUSE—BETHANY

PRUDENCE CRANDALL HOUSE—CANTERBURY

WARNER HOUSE—CHESTER

PLATE XXVII.

XXIX) is a columnar porch of the type which generally serves as a front entrance. Since this latter house is of unusual elaboration throughout, its side entrance cannot be regarded as typical. That of the Gay house is a much commoner form. But many such entrances were still simpler, having only a pilaster treatment, or even nothing more than a moulded architrave. (Plate XXIX.) Because, in houses of the central-hall plan, the side-entrance door opened into the small entry between the front and rear doors (Plate XXIX), a glazed transom above the door was nearly always introduced for the purpose of admitting some light to an otherwise dark space.

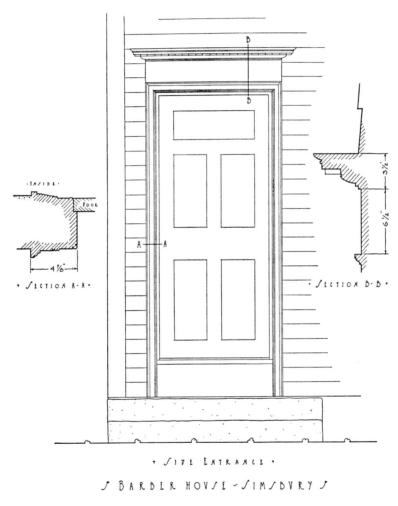

· SIDE ENTRANCE ·

BARBER HOUSE - SIMSBURY

FIGURE 123.

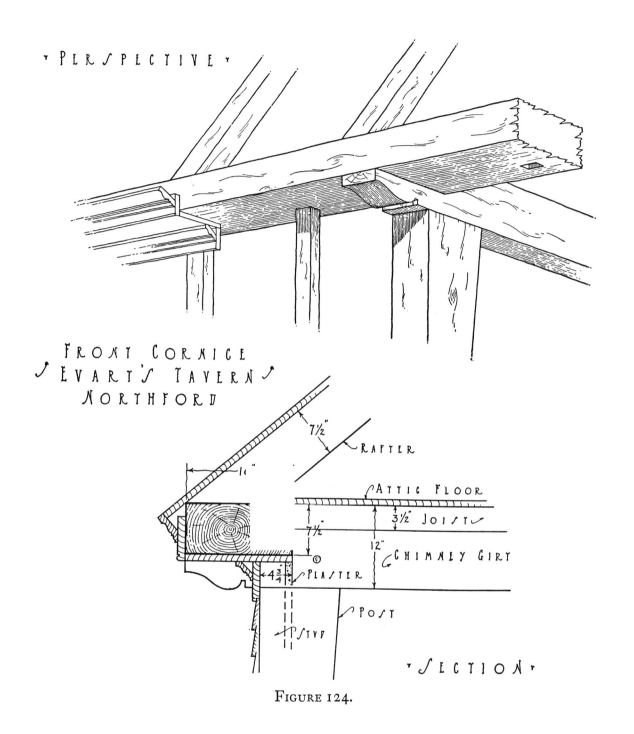

· PERSPECTIVE ·

FRONT CORNICE
EVART'S TAVERN
NORTHFORD

RAFTER

7½"

1"

ATTIC FLOOR

3½" JOIST

7½"

12"

CHIMNEY GIRT

4¾"

PLASTER

POST

STUD

· SECTION ·

FIGURE 124.

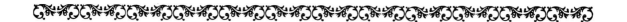

Chapter XII. The Main Cornice

IN the construction of the earliest and most crudely built houses there was probably no attempt at any form of cornice treatment across the front of the house at the eaves. The bevelled ends or "feet" of the roof rafters were allowed to project about twelve inches beyond the plate which supported them, and their covering of boards and shingles served to shed away from the walls of the house the rain water which fell on the roof.

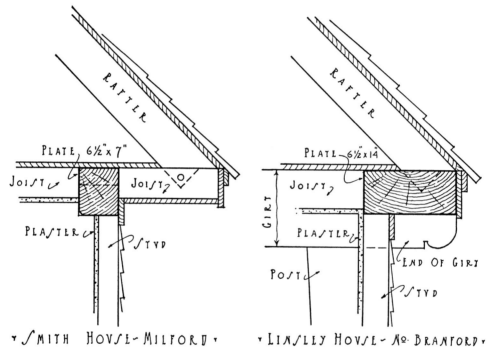

FIGURE 125.

For a considerable period—up to 1700 and even later—this arrangement was continued across the rear of the house; but a more formal method of cornice treatment at the front was of early origin.

Investigation of the earliest cornices which still exist indicated that they were formed in nearly every instance by framing the front plate in such a manner that its outer face extended beyond the house line below it. The front cornice of the old Evarts Tavern in Northford (*circa* 1710) is so built; and its construction is of extreme interest. From Figure 124 it will be seen that the greater part of the front plate, the width of which is more than twice its depth, extends beyond the front wall of the house, its back being flush with the inner sides of the studs. It is supported in this position by the cantilevered ends of the

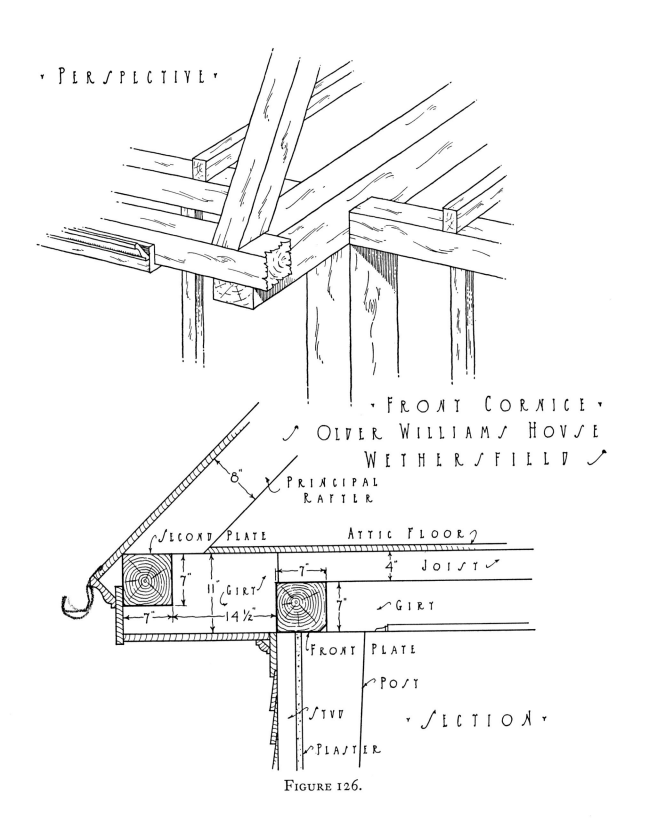

· PERSPECTIVE ·

· FRONT CORNICE ·
ſ OLVER WILLIAMſ HOVſE
WETHERſFIELD ſ

8"
PRINCIPAL
RAFTER

SECOND PLATE   ATTIC FLOOR
7"   4"   JOIST
11" GIRT
14½"   7"
7"   GIRT

FRONT PLATE

POST

· SECTION ·

STVD

PLASTER

FIGURE 126.

ROBBINS HOUSE—ROCKY HILL

CHAFFEE HOUSE—WINDSOR

GENERAL COWLES HOUSE—FARMINGTON

ROBBINS HOUSE—ROCKY HILL

PLATE XXVIII.

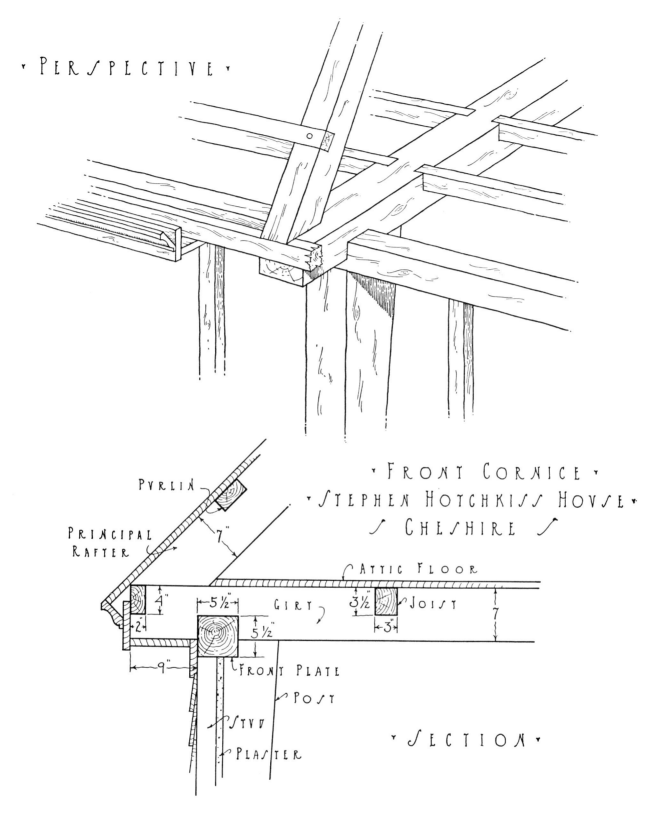

· FRONT CORNICE ·
· STEPHEN HOTCHKISS HOUSE ·
⌐ CHESHIRE ⌐

PURLIN

PRINCIPAL
RAFTER

7"

ATTIC FLOOR

4"

5 ½"

GIRT

3 ½"

JOIST

7

2"

5 ½"

3"

9"

FRONT PLATE

POST

STUD

· SECTION ·

PLASTER

FIGURE 127.

four second-story girts, the projecting ends of which have been hewn into the form of brackets. The plate is cased with wood; so that, with the addition of crown and bed mouldings, a cornice of more or less Classical contour results.

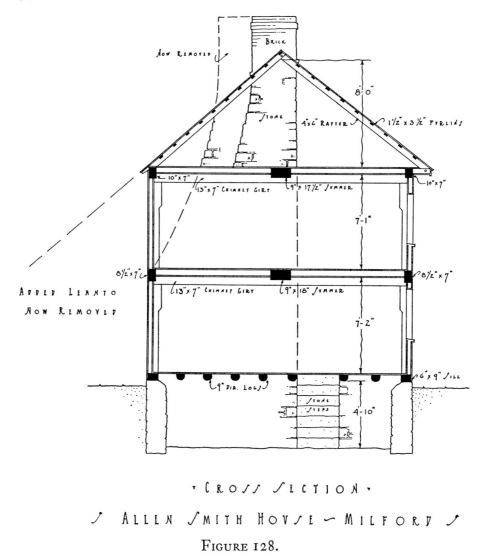

· CROSS SECTION ·

✦ ALLEN SMITH HOUSE — MILFORD ✦

FIGURE 128.

The front cornice of the Linsley house in North Branford (*circa* 1700), shown in section in Figure 125, is quite similar in its construction. As the Evarts Tavern and the Linsley house are within a few miles of each other, it is possible that they are both the work of the same builder. As in the just preceding example, the front plate is extremely wide for its depth, and is projected beyond the house line so that it is flush with the backs of the studs on the inside. The ends of the four girts supporting it, which are cantilevered over the tops of the front posts, have been cut in the form of rather clumsy brackets. This plate is cased on the face, but not on the bottom, which is left exposed; mouldings are altogether

WHEELER-BEECHER HOUSE—BETHANY

CHAMPION HOUSE—EAST HADDAM

GRANT HOUSE—EAST WINDSOR

ELY HOUSE—ELY'S LANDING

PLATE XXIX.

lacking. Both of these cornices, though of decidedly unusual construction, display a common feature in that the front plate is framed out beyond the house line. The purpose of keeping the plate well forward was to provide a foundation upon which the cornice could be built up; and numerous devices of framing were resorted to for this purpose.

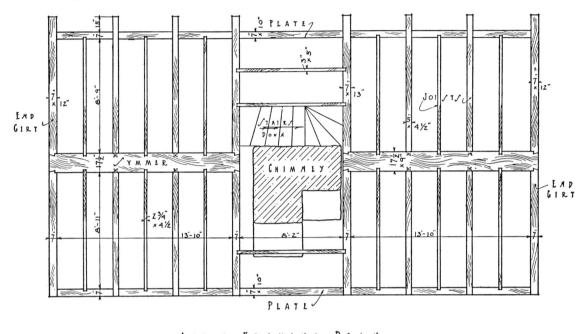

• ATTIC FRAMING PLAN •
∫ ALLEN ∫MITH HOV∫E - MILFORD ∫

FIGURE 129.

The construction of the front cornice of the older Williams house in Wethersfield (*circa* 1680) is shown in Figure 126. Here is the somewhat common arrangement of two front plates, the first on the house line and the second framed out 14½ inches beyond it. The girts which carry the second plate are halved on to the first plate where they cross it. A somewhat similar arrangement is to be seen in the main cornice construction of the Deacon Stephen Hotchkiss house in Cheshire (*circa* 1730), illustrated in Figure 127. Here the expedient of cantilevering the second-story girts was likewise resorted to, although in place of a second plate there is only a small 2-by-4-inch purlin. This purlin served as a foundation or nailing piece upon which the cornice was built up, quite as the second plate did in the older Williams house cornice. (Compare Figures 126 and 127.)

The cornice of the Smith house in Milford (*circa* 1690) is also a constructional one, as a section of its framing shows. (Figure 125.) In building this cornice, the principle of the cantilever was also resorted to; for, although the front plate occupies its accustomed place on the house line, the rafter feet, instead of resting on it, are supported by the projecting ends of the principal attic-floor joists. (See Figures 128 and 129.) These joists are halved on to the plate where they cross it. The projection thus gained beyond the house line is simply cased in, and no mouldings are present. In this respect the cornice is similar to that of the Linsley house. The construction of the Smith house cornice is extremely unusual; the writer has seen none other like it in Connecticut. Across the rear of this house, no form of cornice is to be seen; for the rafter feet, the ends of which are simply bevelled off, project beyond the plate on which they rest. (Figure 53.) Another cornice treatment of exceedingly rare occurrence in Connecticut is that consisting of a plastered cove, as in the Pardee house (*circa* 1725) in the town of North Haven. (Plate V.) My

FIGURE 130.

investigations have disclosed no other work of a similar sort in any other part of the state. This plaster cove extends only across the front and one end of the house; it is shown more clearly in detail in Plate XVII. The outside face of the plate most commonly projects beyond the studs, and is cased in so as to form a simple or box-like cornice. The front cornice of the Norton house in the town of Guilford (*circa* 1690) is of this type, a detail which indicates its early date.

From construction of this sort to the addition of mouldings, with the resultant formation of a more Classical cornice, was but a step. Although the "boxed cornice" is of old form, it unmistakably exhibits the influence of Wren and his school; the note which it echoes is, in a rudimentary form, Classic. The development was quite similar, in a way, to what came to pass when casing was resorted to as a means of finishing or concealing members of construction on the inside of the house, such as girts and summers. By means of thin moulded boards, cornices of more or less Classic contour were built up.

The first cornices in the formation of which mouldings were used were of extreme simplicity. Nothing but straight mouldings were employed, dentil courses and modillion brackets being later introductions. One of the chief characteristics of cornices of this type is the treatment which was nearly always applied to the ends, where they return against the house. This treatment was generally such that the corona or fascia stops flush with the corner boards of the house at either end. (Figure 130.) The projection in front is usually from 10 to 12 inches.

Not until very late—1800 or thereafter—was the cornice returned across the gable ends of the house. Such treatment smacks strongly of the Georgian manner, and is usually associated with a much flattened roof pitch. The gable end thus becomes, in both appearance and treatment, more or less of a pediment, though of course without its supporting orders.

PRUDENCE CRANDALL HOUSE—CANTERBURY

MAJOR TALMAGE HOUSE—GUILFORD

WHEELER-BEECHER HOUSE—BETHANY

BASSETT HOUSE—BETHANY

PLATE XXX.

These were present, in a sense, when a pilaster treatment was employed at the corners of the house. Where the cornice was returned across the gable ends of the house, the pediment-like space above it very often contained a window of semielliptical shape, or one of Palladian form, to admit light to the attic. The Bassett house in Hamden (1819) affords a typical example. (Plate XXX.)

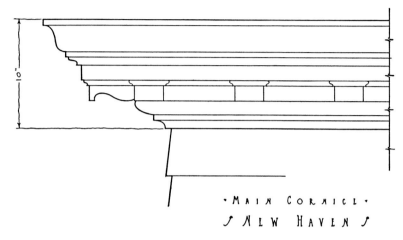

FIGURE 131.

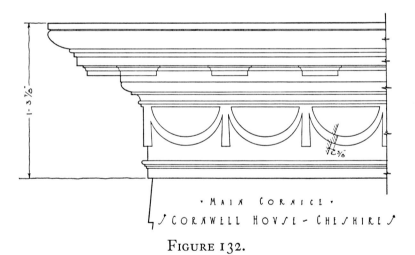

FIGURE 132.

During the latter part of the eighteenth century the main cornice came to be a feature of considerable prominence. An added dentil course, or sometimes two dentil courses, enriched it, as well as additional moulded members; and the introduction of modillion brackets took place. All mouldings entering into the composition became finer in scale, more elegant in profile. A typical cornice of the period is shown in Figure 131.

About 1800, or later, a frieze was very often added beneath the cornice proper, and filled with some form of ornamentation. This was a result of the general search for en-

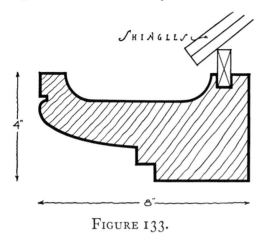

FIGURE 133.

richment which was then taking place. As by that time Adam influence had made itself strongly felt in America, such decoration of the frieze was generally in the form of vertical fluting or reeding, sometimes combined with the familiar festoon motive. This graceful and pleasing form of ornamentation was produced by boring holes of graduated sizes, or by applying "swags" cut from thin boards, which were nailed on to the frieze. The cornice of the Cornwell house in Cheshire (*circa* 1820) affords us an example of the latter treatment. (Figure 132.)

An interesting though not uncommon feature is the formation of a crown moulding and rain-water gutter in combination, from a single solid piece of wood. (Figure 133.) The specimen from which the drawing was made was taken from the cornice of a brick house in the town of North Haven, built in 1756, as figures formed by dark header brick in the gable ends of the structure testify. The wood from which it is made is white cedar; and it became defective only after a hundred and fifty years of faithful service! This rep-

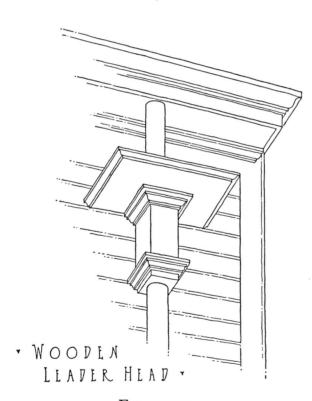

· WOODEN
LEADER HEAD ·

FIGURE 134.

resents what is probably the earliest type of gutter, for the "hanging" variety is quite modern. Generally, no attempt was made to dispose of rain water, which was merely let drip from the eaves. Gutters and leaders were exceptional before 1800. Occasionally, but not often, leaders are to be found which are nothing more than hollow cylinders of wood.

The leader head, likewise made of wood, and embellished with mouldings, appears to be a feature peculiar to Farmington. (Figure 134.) Its use there occurs with considerable frequency, but it is not usually to be met with outside that locality.

In connection with the cornice, we may properly consider the rake, formed at either end of the house by the juncture of the roof with the side walls. In early work, the rake was formed by

BISHOP HOUSE—GUILFORD

STONE HOUSE—GUILFORD

HART HOUSE—GUILFORD

DAVENPORT HOUSE—DAVENPORT RIDGE

PLATE XXXI.

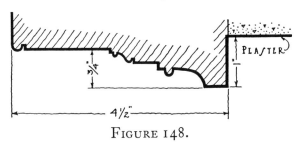

FIGURE 148.

with great ingenuity, to resemble squared columns. The posts in the parlor of the Deming house in Colchester (1771) are so treated. The capitals are of the Ionic order, delicately carved of wood; the shafts are fluted, with an entasis; and the handsomely moulded bases rest upon pedestals having moulded caps and bases and panelled dies. Such elaboration, which also occurs in the Epaphroditus Champion house at East Haddam (1794), is not often to be met with, and is a sign of very late work. It is never found in houses of the central-chimney type.

Girts were often simply cased—the projecting corners having a three-fourths-inch bead like the posts—and the summer similarly treated. The favorite method, however, was, taking advantage of their form, to finish against the plaster ceiling with a *cyma erecta* and small *cyma reversa;* so that the whole combination, including the bed mouldings beneath the girt, appeared as a cornice about the room, at the intersection of walls and ceiling. (Figure 149.) Where mouldings were so used, they were continued along the sides of the summer from the points where it intersected with the girts.

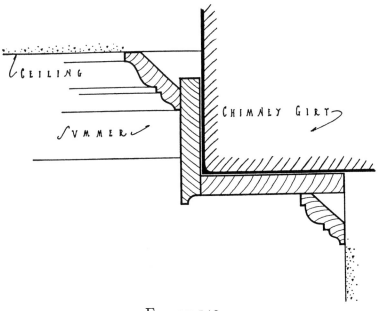

FIGURE 149.

An interesting variation of this scheme is to be found in the living room of the Welles-Shipman house in South Glastonbury (1750), where the mouldings which finish the girts are broken with slight offsets about sixteen inches from their intersections with the summer and the corner posts. So far as has been observed, this is an unique example of such treatment.

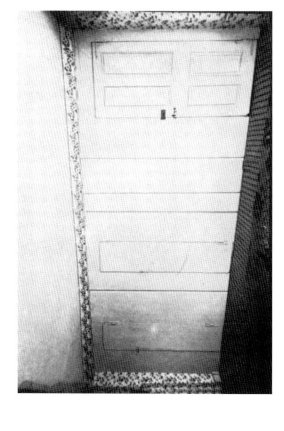

OSBORN HOUSE—SOUTHPORT

WELLES-SHIPMAN HOUSE—SOUTH GLASTONBURY

BIDWELL-MIX HOUSE—WEST HARTFORD

LEE HOUSE—BROOKFIELD

PLATE XXXIII.

The under side or soffit of the summer was rarely finished with an elaborate panel treatment. The reason why such finish is unusual is probably that, by the period when we should expect it to have occurred, the summer had disappeared, or at least shrunk to its late form and ceased to appear below the plastered ceiling. The summers in the parlor of the older Noyes house in Lyme (1756) and in the Warham Williams house in North-

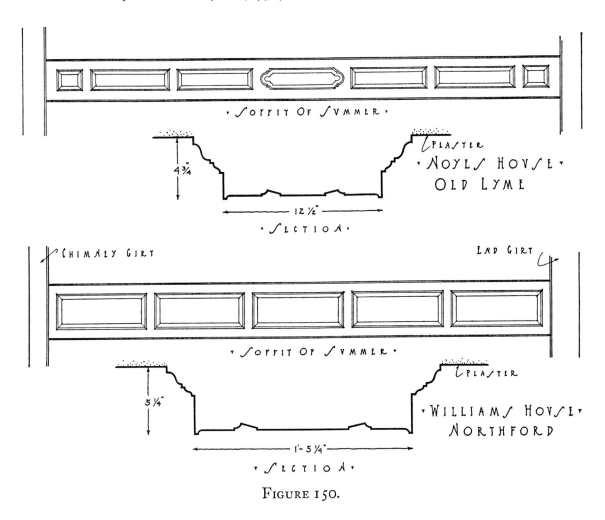

FIGURE 150.

ford (1750) are finely panelled on the under side. (Figure 150.) The treatment of the summer of the Noyes house is of greater elaboration than any which the writer has seen in Connecticut.

Casing of constructive members in this fashion is not to be regarded as necessarily contemporaneous with the building of the house itself: it was often carried out at a much later date.

The treatment of horizontal girts as cornices was sometimes carried to a point of great elaboration. In the aforementioned Deming house in Colchester, this cornice treatment,

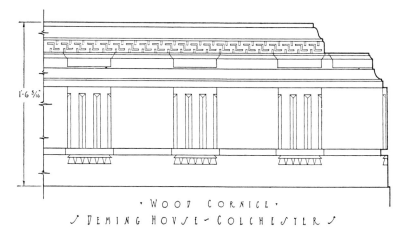

· W O O D   C O R N I C E ·
ſ D E M I N G   H O V ſ E - C O L C H E ſ T E R ſ

FIGURE 151.

· Soffit of Mvtvll ·

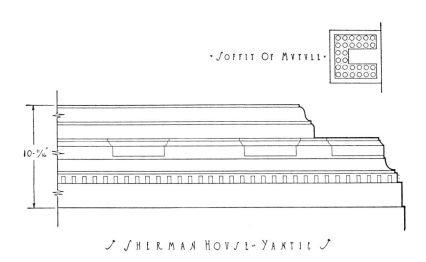

ſ S H E R M A N   H O V ſ E - Y A N T I C ſ

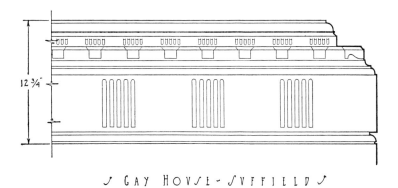

ſ G A Y   H O V ſ E - ſ V F F I E L D ſ

FIGURE 152.

both in the parlor and throughout the central hallway of the first floor, is very handsome. (Figure 151.) The vertical fascia below the crown moulding is carved with a variation of the Greek fret, and delicate modillion brackets are introduced below it, bearing in turn upon a bed moulding carved with the Classic egg and dart. A somewhat similar treatment is to be seen in the Champion house at East Haddam, and in the central hallway of the Sherman house in Yantic (1785) and the Gay house in Suffield (1795). The two last-named examples, however, are much simpler and have no carving. (Figure 152.)

Inside window shutters are occasionally found, though they are by no means common. They are of two types: the folding and the sliding. The folding type, in three or four vertical sections, hinged so as to fold upon themselves on each side of the window opening, either against the jamb or into recesses provided for their accommodation in the wall itself, is the more common of the two. Those of the sliding type were usually made in two sections, each half sliding on a track formed by the chair rail at the bottom and the girt at the top. In

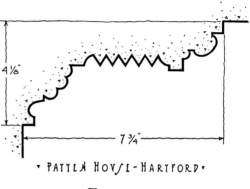

· PATTLA HOVSE - HARTFORD·

FIGURE 153.

some cases these shutters slid into pockets formed in the thickness of the walls and specially constructed to receive them. In the so-called "Beehive" in the town of Andover, and in the Bildad Phelps house at Hayden Station (1780), the shutters are of this variety. Very handsome shutters of the folding type, each section of which is panelled, may be seen in the Governor Trumbull house in Lebanon (1753). The top panels of these shutters are pierced with heart-shaped openings—a feature which, since it admits some light and air, is useful as well as decorative. (See Plate XX.)

Inside shutters are rare, and they do not appear in Connecticut before the middle of the eighteenth century.

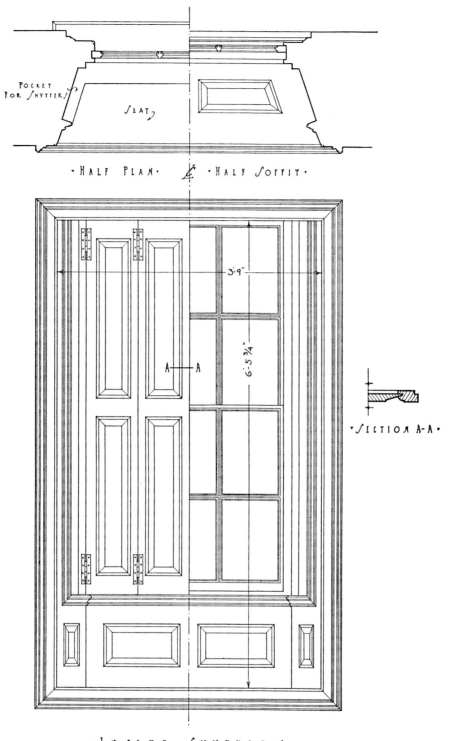

·HALF·PLAN· & ·HALF·SOFFIT·

POCKET
FOR SHUTTERS

SEAT

3'·9"

6'·5¾"

A ——— A

·SECTION A-A·

· INSIDE SHUTTERS ·
S CHAFFEE HOUSE ~ WINDSOR S

FIGURE 154.

SILAS DEANE HOUSE—WETHERSFIELD

MACK HOUSE—HAMBURG

BURBANK HOUSE—SUFFIELD

PHELPS TAVERN—SIMSBURY

PLATE XXXIV.

Chapter XIV. Panelling

BEFORE the advent of plastering, wood wainscot was used for finishing the interior walls of the earliest houses. Some form of covering was necessary for the inside of the house walls, as well as for partitions; and broad pine boards with bevelled or moulded edges, extending in unbroken lengths from floor to ceiling, were used for that purpose. Wainscot was also employed which ran horizontally, both with and without moulded joints.

Of the early Connecticut houses which remain to-day, none is entirely finished on the interior in this manner, though they may have been so originally. The occurrence of even a single room which is wainscoted throughout is rare. But few, if any, of the very earliest houses which remain to us are in their original condition. In nearly every instance changes have been wrought, additions made.

In early work, wainscot was never applied to the ceiling: the joists of the floor above, planed and sometimes beaded, were always left exposed. The use of wainscot was confined, then, to vertical wall surfaces. Occasionally, though very rarely, some wood other than white pine was employed for wainscot. The wainscot on the second floor of the Thomas Buckingham house in Milford, asserted to have been built in 1639, is of butternut; that on the second floor of the Caleb Dudley house in the Town of Guilford (*circa* 1690) is of whitewood. The wainscot of the Dudley house is made up of very wide boards, averaging twenty inches in width, halved together at the joints, which are finished with a very interesting quirk moulding, shown in section in Figure 155.

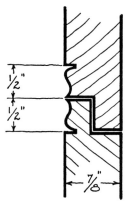

FIGURE 155.

A typical example of the use of wainscot is shown in Figure 156, which is taken from the second floor of the Nathaniel Strong house in East Windsor (*circa* 1700). The vertical joints display the customary bead-and-bevel section, used so commonly later on for panelling—a fact which is responsible for the term "panel sheathing," sometimes applied to such wainscot.

The hall of the Thomas Lee house in East Lyme—the part built in 1664—has walls finished with vertical wainscot, the jointing of which is of the same section. The room above it on the second floor—the hall chamber—is finished in a similar manner. (Figure 157.)

In the Linsley house in the town of North Branford, built *circa* 1700, the only wainscot remaining at the present time is that which covers the fireplace wall of the parlor chamber. (Figure 158.) The white pine boards which entered into its construction are of two widths, thirteen and nineteen inches, placed alternately. The narrower boards have bevelled vertical edges, and the broader ones, which are really stiles, enclose their edges between a rabbet at the back and a quarter-round bead formed on the exterior or visible surface. The same treatment is to be found on the fireplace wall of the parlor of the Tyler house in Branford (*circa* 1710); although the boards there, which are also pine and of similar "panel" section, are much narrower—eight and nine inches.

FIGURE 156.

Later on, wainscot as a form of interior wall covering gave way to plaster, although the use of wood as a covering of the fireplace walls persisted until a late date. Plastering was employed early in the New Haven Colony; but in Hartford and the other towns of the Connecticut Colony, wainscot persisted until 1730 or 1740. Even after the use of plaster for the front rooms of the house had become the rule, wainscot was still used for finishing the walls of the rear rooms, especially the kitchen and the less important rooms of the second floor. In houses of the central-hall type, pine wainscot is occasionally to be found in the middle room of the second floor, which corresponds to the kitchen chamber of the lean-to house, or in the smaller room at either side of it.

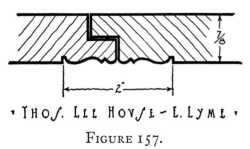

FIGURE 157.

the middle room of the second floor, which corresponds to the kitchen chamber of the lean-to house, or in the smaller room at either side of it.

After plaster had come into common use, wainscot persisted until 1750 or even later, in a much diminished form, beneath the chair rail of the exterior walls. The joints of such wainscot are always horizontal, unless, as in some instances, a regular system of panelling was installed, with rails, stiles, and raised or bevelled panels. The height of such horizontal wainscot above the floor was evidently determined by the height of the window sills above the floor; for the chair rail, or wainscot cap, is generally formed

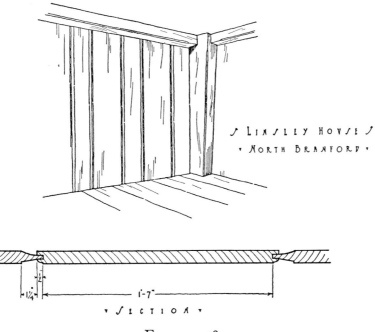

FIGURE 158.

by a continuation of the window stool and of the mouldings beneath it. Even after the use of this type of wainscot was discontinued, the extension of the window stool and its apron, often carved and moulded, and forming a chair rail against the plaster, persisted for a number of years. It is often to be found in houses which were built as late as 1800. The space beneath it, which had formerly been finished with wood, was of course plastered.

When plaster superseded this form of wainscot, it became necessary to finish against the floor with a baseboard, the surface of which was set flush with the plaster. It might almost be said that the original wainscot shrank to the present baseboard. In later examples, the baseboard was projected beyond the face of the plaster, sometimes moulded at the top, and, though rarely, carved, as is that in the

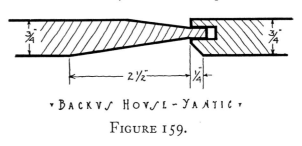

FIGURE 159.

the plaster, sometimes moulded at the top, and, though rarely, carved, as is that in the parlor of the Rectory at Monroe (*circa* 1810). (Figure 161.)

From the use of wainscot on the wall against the chimney to an arrangement of panels held in place by rails and stiles is but a step. Panelling of this type is never to be found in the earliest houses except as a later introduction, though the chests of the period prove

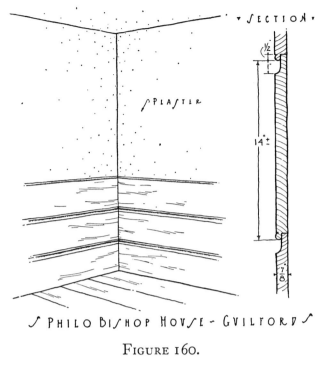

S PHILO BISHOP HOVSE - GVILFORD S

FIGURE 160.

that builders were familiar with it. The simpler wainscot was probably used because it was cheaper and more easily installed.

The panelling of fireplace walls from 1740-1750 onward is nearly always of great beauty and elegance, and forms, in nearly every instance, the most distinctive feature of the house of which it is a part. Even in houses of the central-hall type, where much skill and careful workmanship were expended on the stairs, the treatment of the panelling always remains of surpassing interest.

White pine, free from knots and of clean, even grain, furnished an ideal material for such work. It did not shrink, warp, or check, largely because the wood used was always well seasoned. We cannot fail to admire the accuracy and careful joinery with which this panelling was always done, or to wonder at its perfect condition to-day, after a century or two of existence, too often with abuse.

In the better houses of the central-chimney type, built from about 1740 onward, we may confidently expect to find the fireplace walls of both front rooms of the first floor

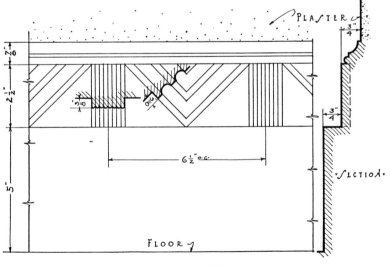

FIGURE 161.

entirely panelled, assuming that the original treatment of those walls remains. Very often the same treatment, though on a less elaborate scale, was carried out in the parlor chamber as well. Although panelling is often to be found in houses of the same type which were built at a much earlier date, it is probably a subsequent addition to most of them.

In the earliest examples of panelling, which were naturally the simplest, the

GRISWOLD HOUSE—BLACKHALL

BELDEN HOUSE—WETHERSFIELD

ELY HOUSE—ELY'S LANDING

RANKIN HOUSE—GLASTONBURY

PLATE XXXV.

16'·0"

7'·0"

· PARLOR PANELLING ·

STORBES OR BARNES HOUSE ~ EAST HAVEN

FIGURE 162.

15'-10"

8'-1½"

▿ PAINTED LANDSCAPE ▿

᷄ WELLES HOVSE ~ LEBANON ᷄

FIGURE 163.

fireplace wall—that next the chimney—was entirely covered with an arrangement, or, more properly, a *composition,* of rectangular panels, secured in place by stiles and rails. (Figure 162.) The fireplace opening was surrounded by a heavy, simple "roll" moulding. No attempt was made at symmetrical arrangement, for the fireplace was rarely on the central axis of the room, and there was always a door on one side of it, opening into the porch. Although the problem of panel grouping seems never to have been worked out twice in the same manner, the result is in every case admirable.

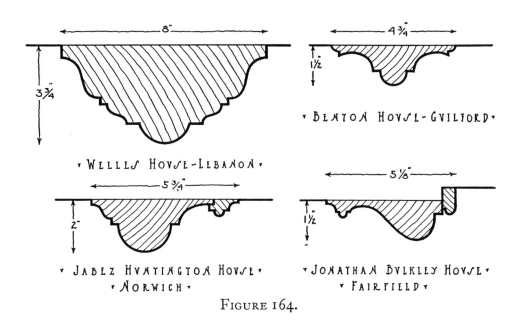

FIGURE 164.

A very early example of panelling is to be found in the parlor chamber of the Welles house in Lebanon (*circa* 1710). (Figure 163.) This panelling, which completely covers the chimney wall, is said to be contemporaneous with the house itself; and although it certainly is very early work, it is doubtful if such an early date can correctly be assigned to it. Owing to alterations carried out some time ago on the first floor, no panelling exists there to-day. In this example, the fireplace opening is framed by a very heavy and somewhat clumsy moulding of bold projection and symmetrical contour. (The earliest mouldings of this sort are nearly always bilaterally symmetrical, whereas the later examples are not. Figure 164.) Above the fireplace of this room is a mantelshelf with bed moulds beneath it, and above that in turn a single large panel, upon which is a painted landscape. Grouped symmetrically on either side are smaller rectangular panels with very broad bevelled edges. They are held in place by heavy bolection mouldings applied to the rails and stiles, so that the panels project beyond them. (Figure 165.) This in itself is a feature of very rare occurrence. The only other similar examples noted are the parlor panelling of the Chaffee house in Windsor, built 1763, and that of the Deming house in Colchester

(1771). In the last named also, the surfaces of the panels project beyond the stiles and rails. Figure 166 shows an interesting comparison between the panel section from the Chaffee house and similar contemporaneous work in England.

The occurrence of a single large panel above the fireplace, held in place by bolection mouldings and projecting beyond the surrounding woodwork, is not, however, uncommon. Often large panels of this type bear landscapes painted upon them in oils, as that in the Welles house.

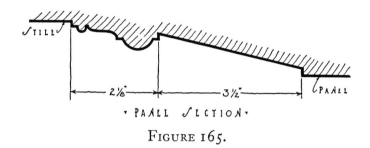

FIGURE 165.

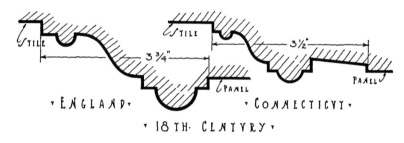

FIGURE 166.

In houses of the central-chimney type of plan, the panelling arrangement was generally simple and dignified. A typical example is that from the Forbes or Barnes house in East Haven (*circa* 1740). (Figure 162.) In later houses, especially those of the central-hall type, the panelling system became much more pretentious and elaborate. The fireplace opening was flanked on either side by fluted pilasters, carried on pedestals with panelled dies, and with caps formed by the mitered bed mouldings beneath the chimney girt, which was treated as a cornice. The parlor panelling of the Taintor house in Colchester (1703), shown in Figure 167, is an example of such treatment. This specimen is unusual because of the form of the upper row of panels, which terminates in a double curve of pleasing contour; also because of the position of the corner cupboard, which has been made a part of the panel system. Panels with this double curve termination are not common; and such work appears without exception to have been confined to the Connecticut River valley. Another example with panelling of this type is shown in Figure 168. This panelling was taken from an old house in Lyme, now demolished.

MANTEL FROM A DEMOLISHED HOUSE—NEW HAVEN

WHEELER-BEECHER HOUSE—BETHANY

TUTTLE HOUSE—GUILFORD

BASSETT HOUSE—HAMDEN

PLATE XXXVI.

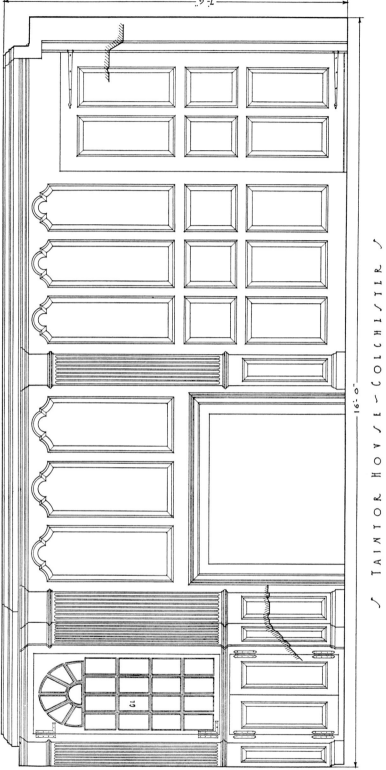

TAINTOR HOVSE ~ COLCHISTER

FIGURE 167.

16'-0"

7'-6"

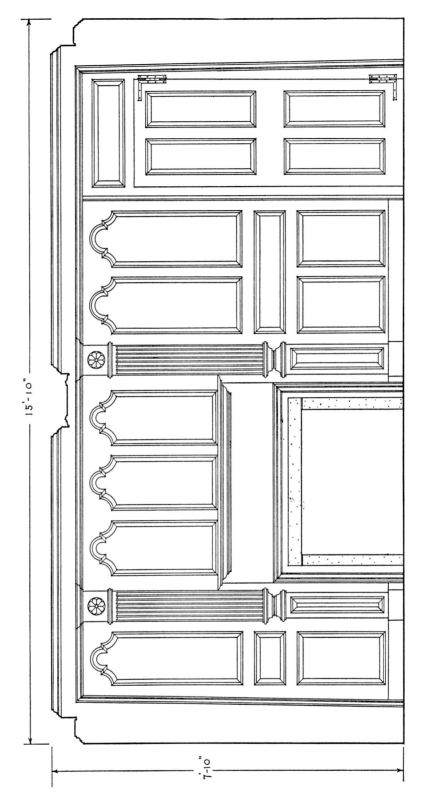

꽃 MATHER HOVSE ~ LYME 꽃

FIGURE 168.

15'-10"

7'-10"

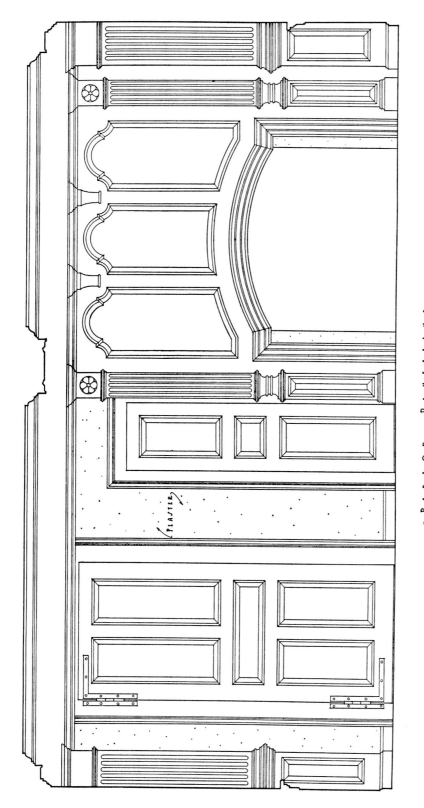

·PARLOR PANELLING·
ʃHAYDEN HOVʃE~EʃʃEX ʃ
FIGURE 169.

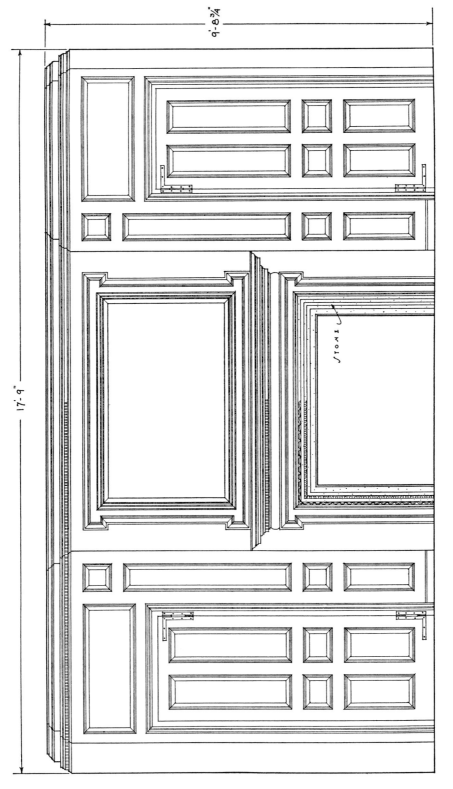

9'-8¾"

17'-9"

STONE

· PARLOR PANELLING ·
⌡ DEMING HOVSE - WETHERSFIELD ⌠

FIGURE 170.

MANTEL FROM A DEMOLISHED HOUSE—
NEW HAVEN

CHAMPION HOUSE—EAST HADDAM

WAID HOUSE—LYME

BARNABAS DEANE HOUSE—HARTFORD

PLATE XXXVII.

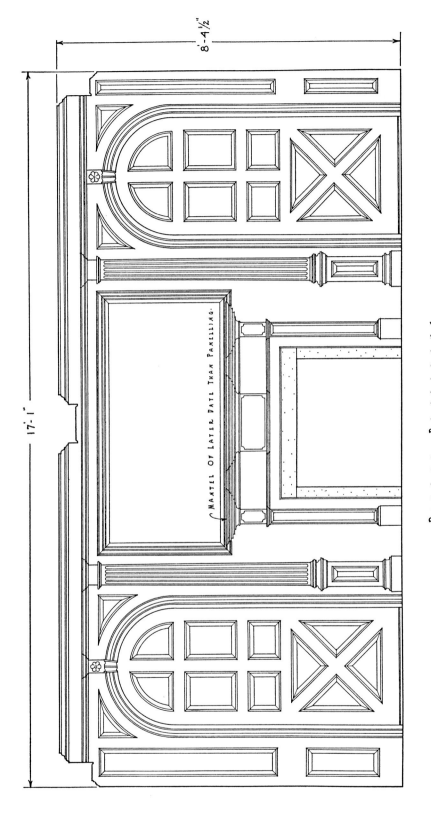

MANTEL OF LATER DATE THAN PANELLING.

8'-4½"

17'-1"

· PARLOR PANELLING ·

WEBB-WILLES HOUSE ~ WETHERSFIELD

FIGURE 171.

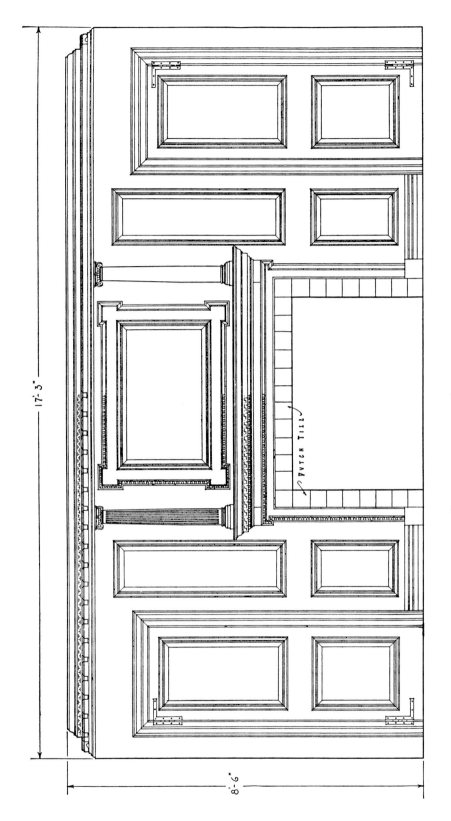

17'-3"

8'-6"

DUTCH TILE

· PARLOR PANELLING ·

DEMING HOVSE ~ COLCHESTER

FIGURE 172.

Two examples of panelled work taken from late houses of the central-hall type are shown in Figures 170 and 171. Both display the characteristics of very late work: the composition has become more formal and perfectly balanced, and all of the detail and scale of moulding is extremely fine. The work shown in Figure 170, from the Henry Deming house in Wethersfield (1790), is in its original condition; the mantelpiece in the Webb-Welles house example (1751) is, however, a later addition. (Figure 171.)

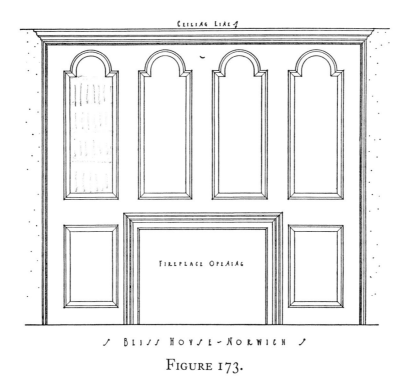

CEILING LINE

FIREPLACE OPENING

BLISS HOUSE - NORWICH

FIGURE 173.

The mantelshelf over the fireplace is sometimes found with bed mouldings beneath it and carrying narrow fluted pilasters between which is a single large panel framed by carved mouldings croisetted at the corners. The panelling of the parlor of the Deming house in Colchester (1771) is one example (Figure 172); and that in the parlor of the Silas Deane house in Wethersfield (1765) is somewhat similar. As in the Webb-Welles house, the fireplace is flanked on either side by doors to china closets or to an adjoining room. Such work is typical of the final development of panelled woodwork. It is interesting to note how the earlier and more informal arrangement gave way to this later expression of more dignified and symmetrical arrangement.

Some of the houses in Norwich exhibit in their panelling an interesting variation from the common treatment, not ordinarily found elsewhere: the formation of a panelled motive around and above the fireplace opening, the remainder of the fireplace wall being simply finished with plaster. (Figure 173.)

With but few exceptions, the panel section is always the same, consisting of a bevelled edge of 1 or 1¼ inches and a quarter-round bead measuring about one-half inch in width. (Figure 174.) Rails and stiles were mortised and tenoned together and secured with wooden pegs, usually two to a joint, about one-fourth of an inch in diameter. Stiles and rails were constructed from inch stock, generally left rough and unplaned on the back or chimney side. The panels themselves were sometimes constructed of thinner material, three-fourths or seven-eighths of an inch in thickness.

The coloring of this old pine woodwork, where it has been fortunate enough to escape the application of paint, is always very beautiful. Through years of exposure to air, light, and smoke from wood fires, it has taken on a rich mellow tone of russet brown and a satin-like sheen—an eloquent plea for leaving this material in its natural condition, for white pine, thus softened and enriched by age, is infinitely finer than it could possibly be under any garb of stain or paint.

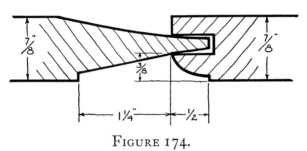

FIGURE 174.

The use of panelled woodwork on the fireplace wall did not persist after 1800. About that time plastering took its place, and builders concentrated their abilities upon the mantelpiece which was applied against it.

Examination of many examples of early plastering reveals the fact that it is generally "one-coat work," and that, although rough in texture and finish, it is of great hardness and evident durability. Shell lime seems often to have entered into its make-up, especially in towns along the Sound, as well as a generous amount of red cattle hair. From the latter fact it may be gathered that Devon or Durham cattle were the principal stock of the colonists. Such specimens of early plaster work are always very rich in lime; and where the source of it was oyster shells, it is common to find good-sized fragments of them, imperfectly calcined, in the plaster.

The earliest specimens of lath are nearly always of oak, sawed in broad sheets three-eighths or one-half of an inch in thickness, split through at intervals with a hatchet, and then spread or stretched out and nailed to the studs in sections. Such lath was similar in form to the expanded metal lath of the present day. The use of individual laths which were separately split or sawed out and applied in the modern manner is of later date.

I have never found in Connecticut an example of plastering applied to wattles, or a woven work of thin twigs, such as was used in England. In the earlier work, the use of split-sheet lath appears to have been the rule. Interior stud partitions which were plastered, though generally characteristic of late work, were of early appearance in the New Haven Colony. As early as 1641 a general court at New Haven established the prices for plastering as follows: "Plastering, for drawing and carrying water, scaffolding, lathing, laying and finishing the plastering, provideing and paying his laborer haveing the lime, clay, sand, hayre, hay with materialls for scaffolding layd neare the place. By the yard for seeling,

WHITMAN HOUSE—FARMINGTON

RANKIN HOUSE—GLASTONBURY

GRISWOLD HOUSE—GUILFORD

WELLES-SHIPMAN HOUSE—SOUTH GLASTONBURY

PLATE XXXVIII.

4-ob, for side walls, being whole or in great paines 4d, betwixt the studs, the studs not measured, 5d-ob, rendering betwixt the studs 2d." It is not probable that the court would have so carefully formulated such a schedule of rates unless plastering were being done to some extent in New Haven at that time. This method of finishing walls and ceilings did not come into general use there, however, until much later—probably about 1735 or 1740. Plastering appeared in Hartford and the neighboring towns of Wethersfield and Windsor shortly before 1700.

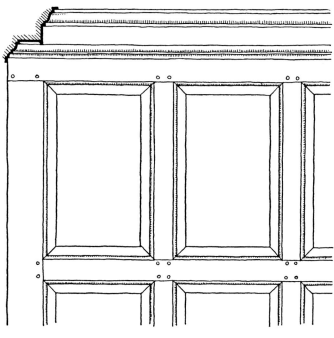

FIGURE 175.

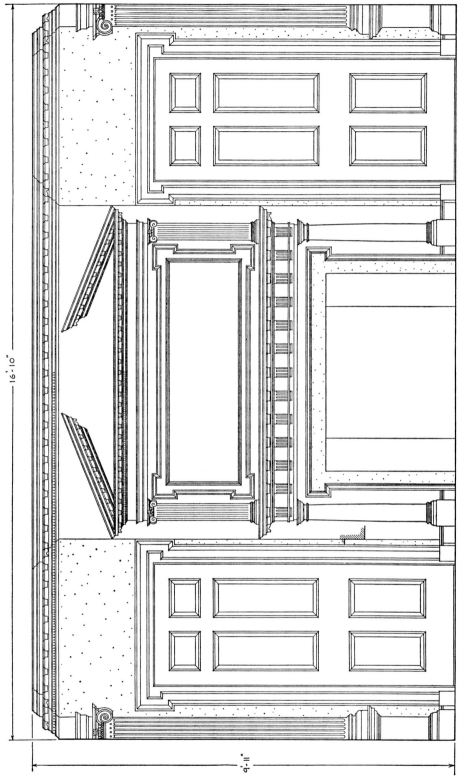

・ F I R E P L A C E   W A L L   O F   P A R L O R ・
ς C H A M P I O N   H O U ς E ～ E A ς T   H A D D A M ς

FIGURE 176.

16'-10"

9'-11"

Chapter XV. Mantels

THE wood finish around the fireplace openings of the earliest houses simply consisted in most instances, as stated in the chapter on panelling, of large, heavy mouldings of bold projection. These mouldings, which were mitered at the corners, formed a frame about the fireplace opening. (Figure 164.) Often called "roll," or, more properly, bolection mouldings, they were generally used until the appearance of the Georgian mantelpiece, after the Revolution.

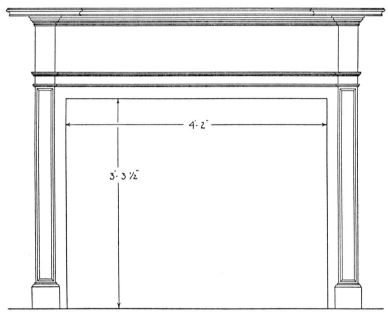

ᒋRᴠᴛʜ Hᴀʀᴛ Hᴏᴠᒍᴇ ~ Gᴠɪʟғᴏʀᴅᒍ

FIGURE 177.

From about that time onward, and especially during the first quarter of the nineteenth century, when it reached its fullest development, this type of mantel, with its typical pilaster arrangement, represented the conventional manner of fireplace treatment. It was repeatedly used in a vast variety of forms, each of which was but a development or variation of a fundamental scheme. The typical arrangement consisted of two pilasters, one on either side of the fireplace opening, supporting an architrave, frieze, and cornice, the top member of which, of exaggerated projection, served the purpose of a mantelshelf. A typical example of this scheme in its simplest form is shown in Figure 177.

It is probable that many of the earlier "roll mouldings" which framed the fireplace openings were removed and replaced by mantels of this type. This change occurred in the parlor of the Webb-Welles house in Wethersfield (1751), where may be seen a mantel of much later date than the panelling to which it has been applied. (Figure 171.) The subsequent introduction of mantelpieces into houses which were originally constructed at a much earlier date is of common occurrence; so that very often a house and its mantelpieces are not contemporaneous.

Mantelpieces of the pilastered type were never used in connection with panelled wainscot except as later introductions; for the Georgian mantelpiece is invariably placed against a plastered background. This simplicity of setting very naturally enhanced the fine scale and richness of detail of such mantels, which were often of extreme delicacy, especially during the period from 1800 to 1815 or 1820.

As may be seen from Figure 177, this type of mantelpiece, in its unelaborated form, consisted of two plain pilasters without entasis, usually of about 4 inches' width and ⅞ of an inch in thickness, placed on high plinth-like bases. The pilaster caps were formed by mitered continuations of the simple mouldings which made up the architrave, above which was placed a plain frieze. This was of considerable height, comparatively speaking: generally eight or nine inches. Vertical breaks, corresponding to the pilasters in width and projection, were carried up through it. About them were mitered the simple bed mouldings of the cornice; and the whole was surmounted by a thin shelf, of six or eight inches' depth, with moulded edges. In the simplest examples the breaks formed by the pilasters were not repeated in this shelf or top member. In more finished specimens the faces of the pilasters were panelled, and also provided with regular moulded bases and capitals along Classic lines. The breaks caused by the pilasters were also repeated in the shelf member, and the edge of the central portion was finished in a gently rounded arc. Such compositions were entirely Classical in feeling and spirit, and they were as strongly indicative of the influence of Wren and his school as was the exterior house cornice of later form.

This fundamental scheme of composition is to be seen in practically all Georgian mantels, elaborate examples of which are to be found, much embellished and enriched with added mouldings, carving, and ornaments in low relief. Small columns, sometimes fluted or beaded and often used in pairs, took the place of the pilasters, which in their turn had become handsomely panelled and provided with conventional capitals and regular bases of regular Attic section. The architrave became of greater height, owing to the addition of more mouldings or members, and the frieze was carved or decorated with *papier-mâché* ornaments such as festoons, baskets of fruit, and dancing figures in low relief. (Plate XXXVI.) A central panel was added to the frieze, which, because of its decoration, became the center of interest of the whole composition. After the influence of the brothers Adam had made itself felt in this country, this central panel was often handsomely carved with the conventional sunburst, which was again repeated in the smaller projections on either side of it, above the pilasters. (Plate XXXVI.) In the simplest as well as the most highly elaborated specimens, the frieze was always higher, or of greater vertical measurement,

TUTTLE HOUSE—GUILFORD

BENTON HOUSE—GUILFORD

OLDER COWLES HOUSE—FARMINGTON

ARNOLD HOUSE—ROCKY HILL

PLATE XXXIX.

than either of the groups of mouldings forming the architrave and the cornice. Because of this predominance in size it very naturally lent itself to various schemes of decorative treatment.

To continue with the cornice: the mouldings above the frieze—those supporting the mantelshelf—became much amplified by the addition of new members of graceful contour and of wide projection rather than great height. Dentils, sometimes beaded, or even drilled with holes, and tiny modillion brackets, were common embellishments. The breaks in the lower members, made necessary by the projection of the pilasters, were carried up and finally repeated in the mantelshelf, as were those above the central panel of the

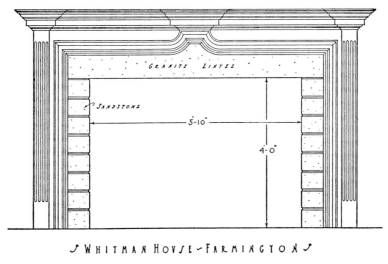

GRANITE LINTEL

SANDSTONE

5'-10"

4'-0"

⌐ WHITMAN HOUSE-FARMINGTON ⌐

FIGURE 178.

frieze. (Plate XXXVI.) The outer edge of the mantelshelf was often further elaborated by being cut in a series of convex and concave curves, very slight, but nevertheless sufficient to add to the general interest of the whole composition.

Skillful design by men whose sense of proportion and scale was exceedingly fine and who possessed a perfect feeling for restraint and elegance of form, coupled with execution of the utmost care, produced mantels many of which are flawless creations. Their grace, beauty, and refinement of detail are too well known and commonly felt to make it necessary to dwell upon these points. The similarity between specimens executed in this country and those which are the product of the Georgian period in England is remarkable; it may be explained, however, by the presence of English workmen here and by the close communication which existed between the two countries at that time.

The exposed masonry of the fireplace, when mantels of this type were employed, was commonly of ordinary red brick, though the old stone hearth was generally retained. Cast-iron firebacks, ornamented with Adam motives in low relief, such as the sunburst or cobweb pattern, are occasionally to be met with, but were never common in Connecticut. When present they are indicative of very late work. In conjunction with the cast-iron fireback in work of a late date, a facing of polished marble is sometimes found about the fireplace opening.

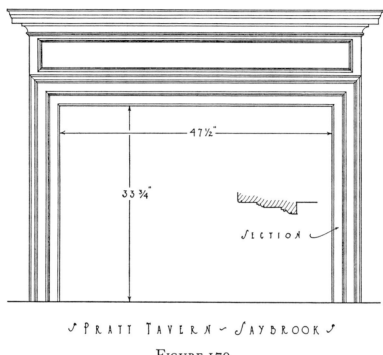

47½"

33¾"

SECTION

PRATT TAVERN ~ SAYBROOK

FIGURE 179.

There never occurred in Connecticut, unless as later importations, mantels showing Dutch influence, with carved or fluted spindles, larger at the top than at the bottom, replacing the customary pilasters or small columns.

As might naturally be expected, the most ornate and elaborately designed mantelpiece is, as a rule, to be found in the parlor. That in the hall or living room is usually less pretentious; and those in the chambers of the second floor are still simpler. Such chamber mantelpieces generally consist simply of a moulded architrave trim around the fireplace opening, with a plain or simply panelled frieze above, surmounted by a few plain mouldings and a shelf. An example of this arrangement is shown in Figure 179, though this particular specimen exists in a room on the first floor.

Mantels of this type are commonly to be found in the kitchen or the old hall, especially in a house of the lean-to period. (Figure 79.)

WHITTLESEY HOUSE—SAYBROOK

McCURDY HOUSE—LYME

KING HOUSE—SUFFIELD

BEERS HOUSE—STRATFORD

PLATE XL.

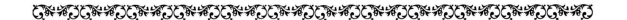

Chapter XVI. Cupboards

THE student of the early architecture of Connecticut cannot but be impressed by the abundance of cupboards in the houses he may examine, as well as by the ingenuity with which, very often, advantage was taken of available space for "cubby-holes" in various nooks and corners. Hardly a panelled fireplace wall exists which has not its complement of cupboards, both large and small.

In houses of the central-chimney type, the diminution in size of the chimney stack above the first floor provided space for such recesses in the panelling; and cupboards accordingly occur oftenest in the upper part of the woodwork, near the ceiling. The panelled doors of cupboards so placed form a part of the whole composition of the fire-place wall. (Figure 162.) These cupboards are generally small and not of great depth; and rarely do more than two occur in a single wall. They were always simply sealed with wood on the inside, and sometimes, if large enough, fitted with one or more shelves. The arrangement of cupboards in the fireplace wall of the original tap-room of the Phelps Tavern in Simsbury (1771) is extremely unusual. A continuous row of shallow cupboards with glazed doors extends across the room, against the ceiling. (Plate XXXIV.)

Because of its prominent position and general beauty of form, the cupboard of chief interest is the corner closet, designed primarily as a place for keeping (and incidentally for showing) the choicest pieces of the family china. Variously referred to in old records as the "bowfat," "boffet," or "buffit"—terms which are corruptions of the English "buffet," the office of which piece of furniture it fulfilled—the corner cupboard belongs exclusively to the central-chimney house. The writer has never found one built into a Connecticut house of any other type.

In a great many instances, the corner cupboard was built in subsequently to the erection of the house. If the house were originally of two-room plan and the corner cupboard was introduced at some later date, its installation generally coincides with the addition of the lean-to.

The corner cupboard is generally to be found in the "best room," or parlor, usually in the right-hand farther corner if we stand with our backs to the fireplace. Occasionally, though not often, it is on the left hand. Its position against the outside wall was, however, well fixed, and its occurrence against the chimney wall is rare. As may be seen from Figure 167, the corner cupboard in the parlor of the Taintor house near Colchester (1703) was built against the fireplace wall; but in that example it forms a part of the panelling system. Closets of this type are also found, though rarely, built into the fireplace wall and flush with it. That in the Benton house, Guilford (*circa* 1760), is an example (Plate XXXIX); and also that in the Beers house, Stratford (*circa* 1710). (Plate XL.)

The corner cupboard is always to be found divided into two parts, an upper and a

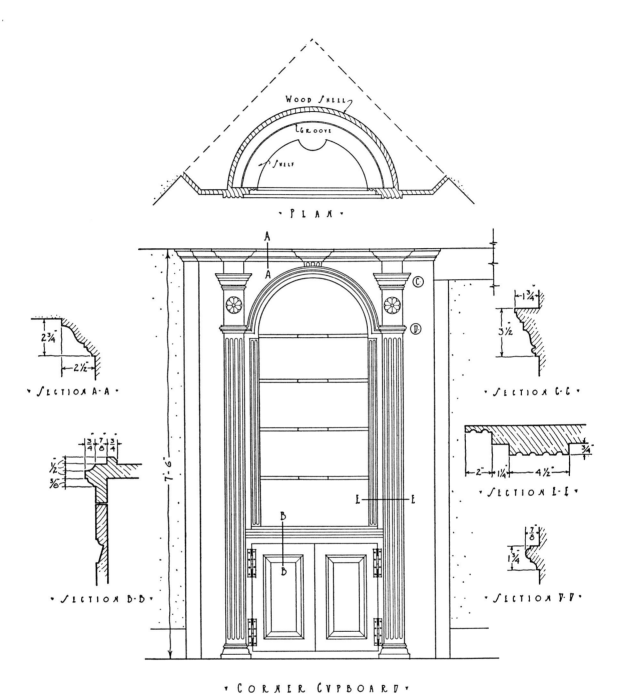

· CORNER CVPBOARD ·

ſ HARRIſON-LINſLEY HOVſE-BRANFORDſ

FIGURE 180.

lower, by a counter shelf, generally placed about thirty inches from the floor. Usually the upper part was enclosed by a single glazed door the width of the opening, below which was a solid wooden door of panelled form. Very often these lower doors occur in pairs. It is not uncommon to find corner cupboards which lack the doors above the counter shelf; *e.g.*, those in the King house, Suffield (*circa* 1774) (Plate XL), and the Harrison-Linsley house, Branford, 1690. (Figure 180.)

Generally, such cupboards as lack upper doors are very early and comparatively primitive specimens. Whether or not the upper door was glazed, the builders were always at great pains, it would appear, to carry out a round-headed treatment. Even when the door was rectangular, the glazing generally terminated in semicircular form. (Plate XLI.) In the great majority of examples, however, the upper door is

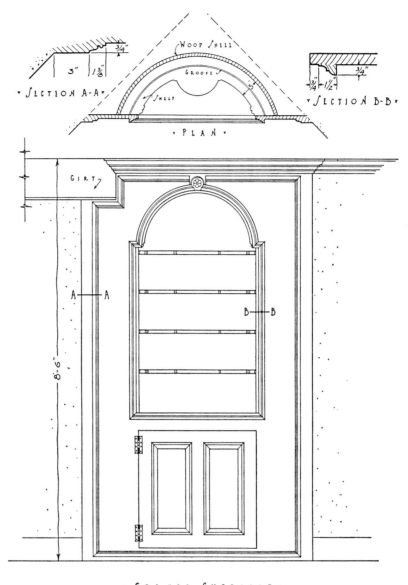

· CORNER CVPBOARD ·

ſ TYLER HOVſE ~ BRANFORD ſ

FIGURE 181.

glazed and has a semicircular head, and the spandrel on either side of it is filled with a panel of the usual type. (Plate XLI.) The diminutive keystone which was set into the trim about the door, at the top of the arch, is a characteristic feature. It is very often to be found decorated with that favored motive, the six-petalled rose, in shallow carving. When a keystone was so used, the mouldings of the room cornice against which it abutted were mitered around it.

When glazed, the cupboard door was invariably made up of small panes of the conventional 6-by-8-inch size, set in broad muntins. These muntins, which were always moulded, were rarely less than an inch in width; some examples measure as much as an inch and a quarter. Since the doors were made of inch stock, the result was a broad flattened muntin, and the glass was necessarily set nearly flush with the inner surface of the door. (Figure 99.)

Another interesting point to be noted in connection with the door of glazed form is the slight offset, usually about one inch, which occurred at the spring of the arch of the glass, without being repeated in the exterior contour of the door itself. (Plate XLI.)

A very unusual muntin arrangement is that of the corner cupboard in the Captain Ambrose Whittlesey house in Saybrook (1799). (Plate XL.) Instead of the customary vertical muntins following the contour of the arch above its spring-line, this semicircular space is divided into three equal parts by two radial bars. The upper part of this cupboard is said to have been taken from an earlier house; certainly it is of comparatively early workmanship.

A form of cupboard which appears to have been peculiar to the town of Guilford has a pair of panelled wooden doors closing the opening above the counter shelf. (Plate XXXIX.) The opening terminates, as may be seen, in the customary round-headed form.

That part of the cupboard opening which was below the counter shelf was always closed, as has been stated, with a solid wooden door or doors. Such doors were nearly always panelled, and in a great variety of forms. If the door were single, its panels were often formed by diagonally crossed stiles. (Plate XLII.) Usually, however, the panels were of simple rectangular form.

In sectional plan, the corner cupboard was generally of semicircular shape or nearly so. The curved back, which extended down only to the counter shelf, was constructed either of wood or of lath and plaster. Both materials were used, it appears, with equal frequency. Occasional examples are to be found in which the back, if built of wood, is carried over into a half-domed termination at the top and carved with radiating flutes into a shell-like form. The corner cupboard in the King house, in Suffield (*circa* 1744), is an excellent specimen of such treatment. (Plate XL.) Shell-topped cupboards, so far from being at all common, may be said to be of comparatively rare occurrence in Connecticut. A very fine example exists in the parlor of the Webb-Welles house in Wethersfield (1751); though there the cupboard is built into the fireplace panelling, and is concealed by a handsomely panelled door, which is flush with the rest of the woodwork.

When the cupboard was across the corner of the room, its face rarely ran directly from wall to wall: it was usually set out, or away from the walls on either side, by an offset of five or six inches. In the later and more elaborate examples, a flat pilaster with shallow fluting was placed on either side of the door opening. (Plate XLII.) In some examples such pilasters extended from floor to ceiling; in others they were supported on pedestals with moulded caps and bases and panelled dies. A common arrangement was to rest the pilaster bases on the counter shelf. The employment of pilasters, which are very primitive in form,

TYLER HOUSE—EAST HAVEN

WELLES-SHIPMAN HOUSE—
SOUTH GLASTONBURY

ROBBINS HOUSE—ROCKY HILL

COMSTOCK HOUSE—EAST HARTFORD

PLATE XLI.

in the corner cupboard of the Talcott Arnold house in Rocky Hill (1764) is of notable interest. (Plate XXXIX.)

The shelves in the upper part of the "boffit" were usually placed about eight or ten inches apart. They were narrow—rarely more than six inches wide—and, like the back of the cupboard, semicircular. Very often the termination of the shelf at either end was cut in an ornamental manner, and a rounded projection was introduced in the center, in order to provide a greater width of shelf for the display of some large object. It was customary to cut a continuous groove along the center of each shelf, so that plates could be stood on edge without slipping.

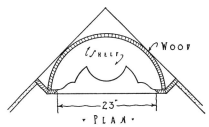

The occurrence of regular closets in houses of the central-chimney type is rather unusual except on the second floor, where they are sometimes found opening from the two front chambers, and built into the space of the chimney bay. (Figure 15.) The decrease in size of the stack on the second floor provided this space, which was sometimes so utilized. In houses of this type in which the stairs to the cellar were not placed beneath those to the second floor, the space beneath the stairs served as a closet, entered by a door from one of the front rooms. An unusual arrangement existed in the Captain Charles Churchill house in Newington, built in 1763, and now demolished. A door beneath the front stairs opened from the porch into a closet-like space between them and the chimney stack, which was utilized as a saddle room. Stout wooden pegs driven into the walls provided safe resting places for equipment too valuable to be left in the barn.

The house of central-hall type, with its two chimneys, each of which was centrally located between a front and a rear room, had, as may be seen from Figure 16, four spaces on each floor which were of the depth of the chimney stack. Closet room was therefore abundant. It is rather unusual, though, to find all such space con-

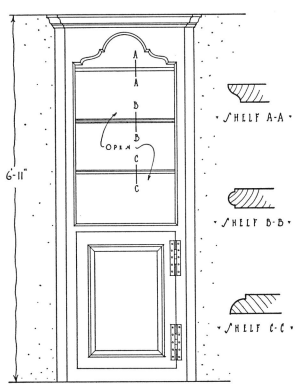

FIGURE 182.

verted into closets: much of it was used for communication between front and rear rooms, or, on the first floor, as a vestibule to a side door.

The modern necessity of having a multitude of closets was evidently not felt by the early builders, probably because their mode of living was simpler and their possessions were fewer than ours of to-day.

We hear much about secret closets, but their actual occurrence is a rarity. One is said to have existed in the space about the chimney stack on the second floor of the older Silliman house in Fairfield (1760). Entered by removing one of the boards at the end of a closet which opened from the hall chamber, it served as a hiding place during the Revolutionary war. A curious closet exists on the second floor of the Acadian house in Guilford (1670). Consisting merely of the space in front of the central chimney stack and behind the stairs, it is accessible by a door from either front chamber. Though referred to as a secret closet, it does not seem to justify that title. What it provided was a secret passage from one room to the other.

CUPBOARD IN AN OLD HOUSE—
SIMSBURY

CUPBOARD IN AN OLD HOUSE—
WEST HARTFORD

BEARDSLEY HOUSE—HUNTINGTON

JUDSON HOUSE—STRATFORD

PLATE XLII.

Chapter XVII. The Stairs

IN the earliest or one-room type of plan, exemplified by the Thomas Lee house in East Lyme (1664) in its first stage, the stairs occupy the front end of the chimney bay, at one side of the single room of the first floor. (Figure 1.) When the plan changed to one of two rooms, the stairs remained in the same place; that is, in front of the chimney, which had now become centrally located. In the lean-to type, the same arrangement held good; for the porch, or space apportioned to the stairs, had become definitely fixed in its relation to the chimney. The rule, then, became established, in houses of the central-chimney type, that the front or main stairs should occupy a position directly behind the front entrance, in front of the chimney stack. Through long adaptation to this space, they became standardized in dimensions and type.

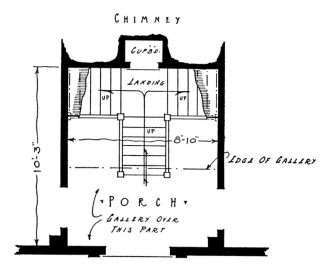

FRONT STAIRS
DEMING HOUSE-FARMINGTON

FIGURE 183.

The space given them was necessarily small, the average chimney bay being about one-half the width of the bays or rooms adjoining it on each side. Accordingly, risers were high and treads narrow. The use of "winders," or diagonal steps at the turns, a common feature of the earliest examples, is one of their distinguishing characteristics. It is possible that some of the first stairs were built entirely of winders, though few such specimens have come down to us to-day. This is not to be wondered at, for a staircase which has no straight runs is both uncomfortable and dangerous to negotiate. In the New Haven Colony the chimney bay was generally of more generous proportions than elsewhere in the state, sometimes by as much as two feet; and this fact, by permitting wider treads, resulted in decreasing the steepness of the stair pitch in houses of that locality.

A front stair arrangement which is comparatively rare and of great interest is that illustrated in Figure 183. The stairs are in the usual space—in front of the chimney stack— but instead of ascending in the usual fashion, they begin directly opposite the front entrance and branch right and left from a landing about halfway up. Doors directly at the top of each flight communicate with the hall and parlor chambers respectively; and access from one room to the other is by means of a gallery above the porch at the second floor level.

It is extremely unusual to find a house of central-chimney plan in which the main stairs are in any other than the conventional position. But the first-floor plan of the Brockway house near Hamburg (*circa* 1725) shows that the main staircase occupies a very unusual place—at the rear of the house. (Figure 184.) Yet it is not of the back-stairs type, but is carefully and somewhat elaborately built, with well-turned balusters and a moulded hand-rail. (Plate XLIII.) From first glancing at the plan of the Samuel Webster house (1787) in East Windsor Hill (Figure 185), it would seem that a similar arrangement existed there. But here the *only* stairs to the second floor are the back stairs, which are enclosed with pine wainscot and have no hand-rail. This is a brick house, only a story and a half in height.

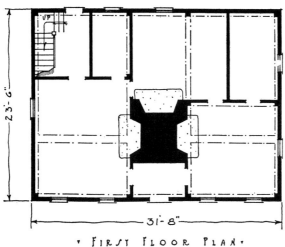

· FIRST FLOOR PLAN ·

♪ BROCKWAY HOUSE - HAMBURG ♪

FIGURE 184.

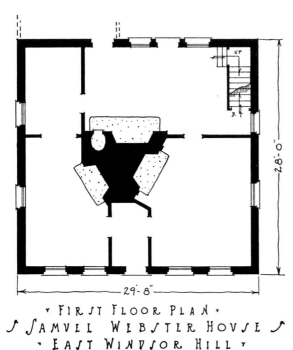

· FIRST FLOOR PLAN ·

♪ SAMUEL WEBSTER HOUSE ♪
· EAST WINDSOR HILL ·

FIGURE 185.

There appears to have been no fixed rule as to whether the stairs were made right- or left-handed. (Right-handed stairs are those which have the hand-rail on the right-hand side, so that the person ascending them turns to the right; left-hand stairs reverse this arrangement.) Right- and left-handed stairs appear to have been of equally frequent occurrence, possibly because their direction was determined by the orientation of the house, which in Connecticut followed no rule. In Rhode Island the early house invariably faced south; but in Connecticut the builders always faced their houses on the main highway, so that, whatever the orientation of the house, the hall, or living room, was placed on the warmer and less exposed side. Inasmuch as the stairs to the cellar, when they existed in

BROCKWAY HOUSE—HAMBURG

PARDEE HOUSE—MONTOWESE

HILL HOUSE—GLASTONBURY

OLDER WILLIAMS HOUSE—WETHERSFIELD

PLATE XLIII.

a house of two-room plan, usually led downward from the hall, the stairs to the second floor were started from the opposite side of the porch, in order to provide the necessary head-room for them. This is why the great majority of stairs in central-chimney houses begin on the side of the porch which is nearest the parlor. Even when, as in the lean-to type of plan, the cellar stairs no longer lead from the hall, this arrangement still persisted.

A feature of common occurrence in the earliest examples of front stairs—one found with sufficient frequency to be counted as a characteristic—is the diminution in height of the last or top riser of the flight. The reason for this is not clear. In the simplest and earliest types of stairs, hand-rails and balusters were lacking, and the whole flight was enclosed by a single thickness of wainscot, generally displaying the familiar panel section and

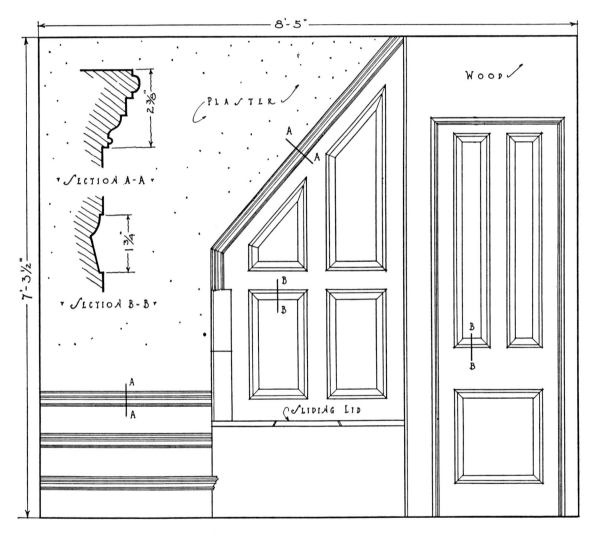

Capt· Lee House - Guilford

Figure 186.

running vertically. The front stairs in the older Bushnell house (1678-1679), near Saybrook, are of this arrangement. (Figure 3.) The use of panelled wainscot below the handrail partially to enclose the stairs is illustrated in Figure 186. Treatment of this sort is decidedly out of the common; the writer has not seen similar work elsewhere in Connecticut.

The next development is the omission of the enclosing wainscot and the introduction of plain square newels and a rail. The open end of the stairs—*i.e.*, the part away from the chimney—was covered by a continuous or box string, in the treatment of which mouldings early came into use. (Figure 187.) The space below the string was covered with simple wainscot, and later came to be panelled. The front stairs of the Moulthrop house in East Haven, shown in Figure 188, are characteristic of this period.

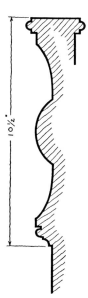

In the third or final stage, the newel posts were often turned and finished with moulded caps. Some of these caps were formed by the mitered intersections of the hand-rail. (Figure 189.) Balusters, nearly always turned, were placed upon the heavily moulded box string, and were at first spaced rather widely apart, with no fixed relation to the stairs themselves. A characteristic feature is the use of half balusters against the newels. (Figure 190.) (Plate XLIV.)

The use of turned balusters began about 1700, the earliest forms being characterized by their squatness and general stumpiness. (Plate XLIII.) Early balusters were generally made up of a great number of very full forms, and their composition was often Jacobean in spirit. From balusters of this sort the development was toward longer and more graceful, flowing

FIGURE 187.

lines, with comparatively few members, as shown in Figure 191. A comparison of typical early and late types, as illustrated in Figure 192, is of striking interest. The front stairs of the Pardee house in North Haven, built about 1725, and those of the older Williams house in Wethersfield (*circa* 1690) display very short balusters of robust form, with a decidedly Jacobean flavor. (Plate XLIII.) In both instances the balusters are placed above vertical pine wainscot which shows the familiar bead-and-bevel section at the joints.

Although most stairs in central-chimney houses display the boxed string, upon which the balusters were equally spaced, now and then occurs a staircase which has an open outer end, with the balusters placed in pairs upon the returned nosing of each tread. (Plate XLV.) This scheme was not altogether fortunate, for it resulted in crowding together the two balusters next the newel post.

Flat balusters, with a contour on two edges produced by sawing, such as may be found in Rhode Island, are a rarity in Connecticut. They are not to be met with west of New London. Balusters of simple rectangular section are not common: it is evident that, even in very early days, the turned baluster was in high favor. A typical example of plain balusters may be seen in the front stairs of the Ezra Griswold house in Guilford (*circa* 1760), shown in Figure 193.

SEWARD HOUSE—GUILFORD

GENERAL WALKER HOUSE—STRATFORD

GENERAL JOHNSON HOUSE—GUILFORD

HYLAND-WILDMAN HOUSE—GUILFORD

PLATE XLIV.

A species of hard pine appears to have been the favorite material for baluster construction, even when the rails and newels were of oak. This preference was possibly due to the greater ease with which such softer wood could be turned upon the lathe. Oak balusters are occasionally to be met with, as in the Hyland-Wildman house in Guilford (*circa* 1660) (Plate XLIV) and the Graves house in Madison (1675).

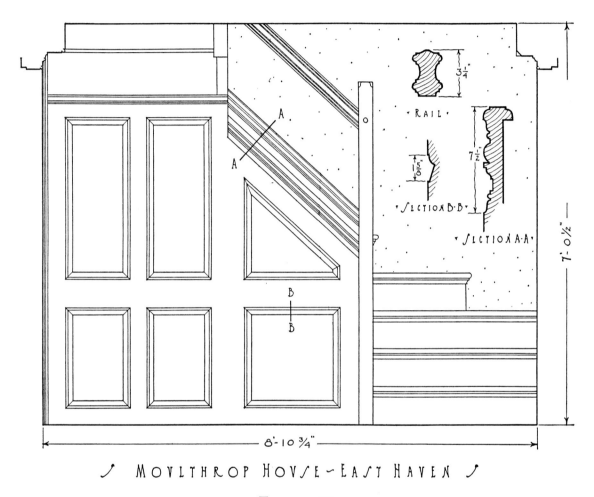

$$\mathcal{S} \text{ MOVLTHROP HOVSE-EAST HAVEN } \mathcal{S}$$

FIGURE 188.

By comparing different specimens, the development of the hand-rail may be traced. The various examples group themselves into three general classes. (Figure 194.) The first type was of simple rectangular section, chamfered slightly at the corners or rounded on top. The next step was marked by the use of mouldings, usually on the outer side, away from the stairs, so that the rail is unsymmetrical in section. The third and ultimate stage is marked by the moulded rail of symmetrical type and greater elaboration. Hand-rails of this last sort are typical of the last period of stair construction in both central-chimney and central-

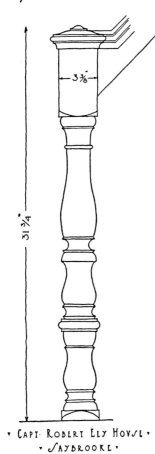

· Capt· Robert Lee House ·
· Saybrooke ·

FIGURE 189.

hall houses. Specimens of the first two groups, but rarely of the last, may often be found made of oak. Hard pine, and, in the latest houses, mahogany, were the woods employed in making the moulded symmetrical rail.

In stairs of the earliest type, which have no hand-rails and are enclosed by wainscot, a square oak post of three- or four-inch section is commonly found at each angle or corner of the stairs farthest from the chimney, into which post the diagonal treads or "winders" are framed. When wainscot was superseded by hand-rails and balusters, these posts remained and served the same purpose. Two more were added: one each at the top and bottom of the flight, to receive the ends of the hand-rail. In most instances the rail is to be found tenoned into the newels and secured with wooden pins. In stairs of central-chimney houses the writer has never found the rail fitted with ramps and ease-offs, such as are common in the stair treatment of late houses of the central-hall type. A customary arrangement was simply to butt the ends of the hand-rail against the newel posts; although occasionally it is found, at the bottom of the flight, mitered into a short level section, which is in turn mitered around the top of the newel post to form its cap. (Figure 195.) This last scheme was the precursor of the ease-off, which was formed by curving the lower end of the rail so that it became level at its intersection with the newel post. Work of this sort could be done, of course, only by a skillful joiner.

The Stowe house in Milford (1685-1690) exhibits a stair treatment of very unusual form and extreme interest. The stairs of this house, which is of irregular plan, are of the "dog-legged" type; that is, the hand-rails of each of the two ramps stop against the same side of a common newel post.

By far the greater number of newels were of plain form and not larger than three or four inches square, and their only ornamenta-

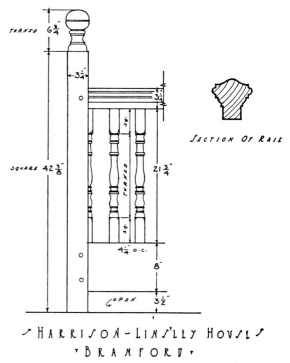

Section of Rail

· Harrison-Linsley House ·
· Branford ·

FIGURE 190.

tion consisted of a simply moulded or turned cap. Newel posts turned throughout their length are less common, although they are frequently found in stairs of central-hall houses. Rarely do we meet with the newel of rectangular section, panelled on all four sides or even, like that shown in Figure 196, only on the front one. In this example, the panel is carved directly into the post, which is of oak. The newel post of the main stairway of

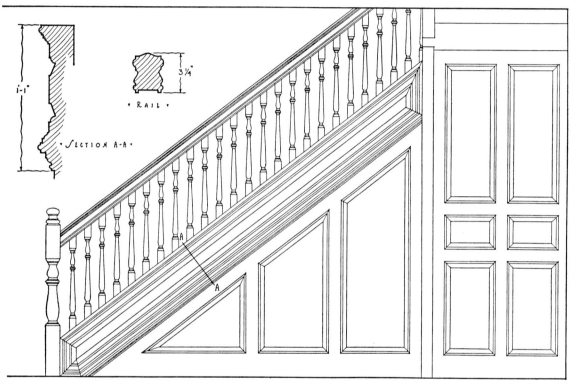

· RAIL ·

· SECTION A-A ·

A

A

ʃ RVʃʃELL HOVʃE ~ ʃTRATFORD ʃ

FIGURE 191.

the Deacon John Benjamin house in Milford (*circa* 1750), illustrated in Figure 197, is unusual in its treatment. Like that of the Bushnell house, it is made of oak. In certain instances the newel was formed by grouping together four balusters, over which the rail was mitered to form a cap.

Occasionally the lower end of the post at the top of the flight is to be found projecting below the finished ceiling of the porch. Where this occurs, the newel usually terminates in a series of handsomely turned mouldings, as does that in the General Walker house in Stratford (*circa* 1740), shown in Figure 198. The same treatment is to be seen in the Coit house in Norwich (1785) and the Governor Trumbull house in Lebanon (1740); but

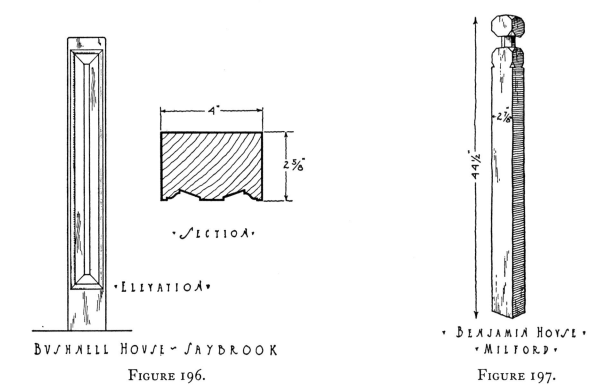

·SECTION·

4"

2⅝"

·ELEVATION·

BVSHNELL HOVSE - SAYBROOK

FIGURE 196.

·BENJAMIN HOVSE·
·MILFORD·

44½"

2⅞"

FIGURE 197.

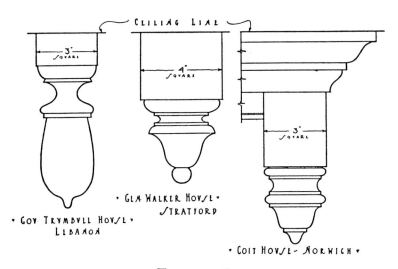

·CEILING LINE·

3" SQVARE

4" SQVARE

3" SQVARE

·GOV TRVMBVLL HOVSE·
LEBANON

·GEN WALKER HOVSE·
STRATFORD

·COIT HOVSE - NORWICH·

FIGURE 198.

Ramps and ease-offs in the hand-rails of these late stairs are rather frequent. In very late work, the termination of the hand-rail at the bottom of the flight was often of helical form, and was supported by an attenuated newel, generally in the form of a small column, about which the balusters were ranked on the first tread. The stairs of the Barnabas Deane house in Hartford (1778) exhibit such an arrangement. (Figure 199.)

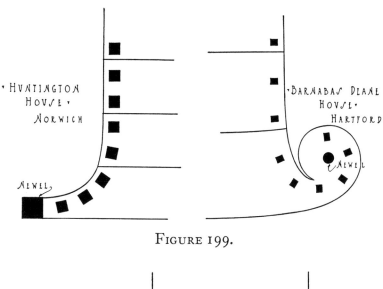

FIGURE 199.

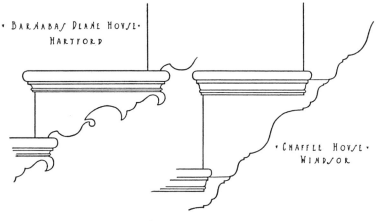

FIGURE 200.

In work of this period, panelled wainscot applied to the stair wall, at the same height above the treads as the hand-rail, is very often a feature of houses which pretend to any degree of elegance. The upper edge of such wainscot, which is moulded, commonly parallels the contours of the hand-rail. (Plate XLV.) It is not unusual to find the curves of the ramps and ease-offs, where these are present, followed out.

Certain features common to stairs of central-chimney houses, persisting until a late date, reappear in stair work of central-hall houses. For example, when the box string gave way and the moulded edges of the treads, together with the mouldings beneath them,

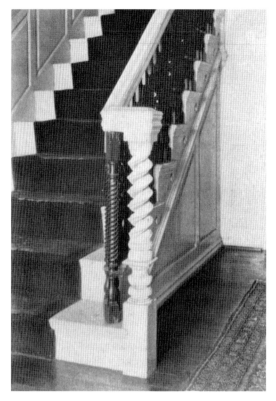

GRANT HOUSE—EAST WINDSOR

GRANT HOUSE—EAST WINDSOR

WEBB HOUSE—WETHERSFIELD

SILAS DEANE HOUSE—WETHERSFIELD

PLATE XLVI.

were returned against the string, a common decorative feature was the scroll-shaped bracket, cut out of thin wood and applied beneath them. (Figure 200.) These brackets are to be found in an almost endless variety of forms; it appears that a different outline was designed for each staircase. The usual thickness of the material from which such brackets were cut is about one-half inch. The contour of such brackets was so designed that the outline of each is a continuation of those above and below it. (Figure 200.) The boxed form of staircase, with the under side of the treads and risers panelled, was apparently not used in Connecticut.

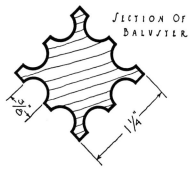

DR. RICHARD NOYES HOUSE-LYME

FIGURE 201.

Hand-rails of late staircases did not vary greatly in section from the forms established in front-entry stair work. The use of a rail of unsymmetrical section, moulded on one side only, is, however, rare in central-hall houses, though it does occur occasionally, as in the Coit house in Norwich (1785).

An unusual treatment of the stairs may be seen in the Dr. Richard Noyes house in Lyme (1814). A half rail, with half balusters below it, has been applied to the plaster wall, repeating the rail and balusters of full section on the open side of the stairs. (Plate XLV.) The balusters of this staircase are quite uncommon in form. They are square in sec-

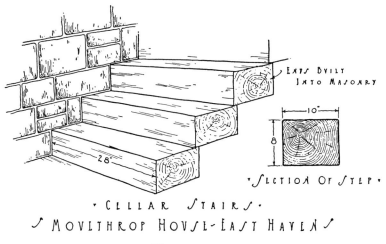

CELLAR STAIRS
MOULTHROP HOUSE-EAST HAVEN

FIGURE 202.

tion, set diagonally upon the treads, and each side is channelled with two vertical flutes. (Figure 201.) Balusters of a similar section were used in the Judge William Noyes house in the same town (1756).

Back stairs came into existence at the time of the lean-to addition. In houses of central-chimney plan they are commonly found at one end of the kitchen, between it and the buttery or the corner bedroom. These stairs were always enclosed, usually with vertical wainscot; and they were purely utilitarian, no ornamentation ever being lavished on them, as it was on the front stairs. Once the back stairs became established, the space beneath them was utilized for stairs to the cellar, which had hitherto been situated beneath the front stairs, leading downward from the hall. Cellar stairs accessible through a door opening into the stair porch are very rare.

·CELLAR STAIRS·

·BECKLEY HOUSE-BERLIN·

FIGURE 203.

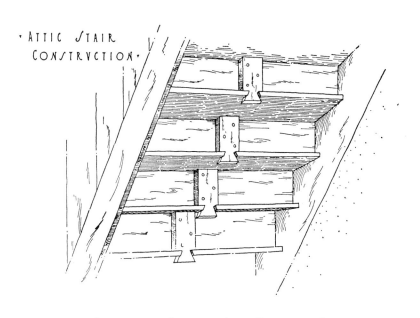

·ATTIC STAIR CONSTRUCTION·

/ PIERPONT HOUSE-NEW HAVEN /

FIGURE 204.

Cellar stairs of the earliest type, such as occur in front of the chimney stack in houses of two-room plan, were of either stone or solid oak logs. When made of logs of rectangular section, like those in the Moulthrop house in East Haven (*circa* 1690), they were generally

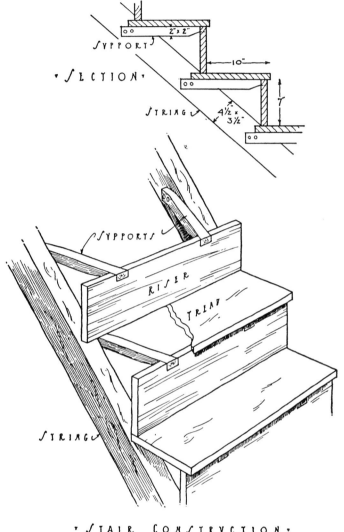

· STAIR CONSTRUCTION ·
S BVSHNELL HOVSE - SAYBROOKS

FIGURE 205.

built into the masonry walls which enclosed them on either side. (Figure 202.) Some houses, such as the Thomas Lee house in East Lyme (1664) and the Beckley house near Berlin (*circa* 1685), have cellar stairs made of solid oak logs of triangular section, secured with wooden pins to heavy string pieces. (Figure 203.) Solid wooden steps are rare, and but few specimens remain to-day. Work of this sort has a distinctively English flavor.

(A cottage in Upper Midhope, England, has a flight leading to the second floor, built of oak logs of triangular section, carried on wooden stringers hewn from heavy logs.) The Graves house in Madison (1675), the Linsley house in North Branford (*circa* 1700), and the Allen Smith house in Milford (*circa* 1690) all have stone steps leading down to the cellar, in front of the central chimney stack. This form of construction is not often found; where it exists, it is a sign of early work. Later types of cellar stairs were simply built of sawn lumber, and have no features of special interest.

J H A W L E Y H O V J E - M O N R O E J

FIGURE 206.

Attic stairs were likewise of simple construction, and in central-chimney houses are generally to be found above those which give access to the second floor. This is especially true of houses which have an added lean-to. When above the main stairs, they are separated from the hallway of the second floor by a wainscot partition, and there is, of course, a door at the foot of the flight. Occasionally such stairs are fitted with a simple hand-rail. Attic stairs are very commonly to be found in the rear part of the house—generally at one end of the kitchen chamber when the house is of the central-chimney plan and has two full stories. Attic stairs also occupy the same position in central-hall houses.

The attic stairs of the Cyrus Hawley house in Monroe (*circa* 1740) consist of a flight of stone steps built against one side of the central stone chimney and leading up from the lean-to attic. (Figure 206.) The steps are very steep. Each is a single block of stone. The stones of the chimney stack are laid in clay, and the steps are bedded in the same material. A similar arrangement exists in the Buckingham house near Huntington (*circa* 1740), not far from Monroe; and such construction being most unusual, it is probable that both houses are the work of the same builder.

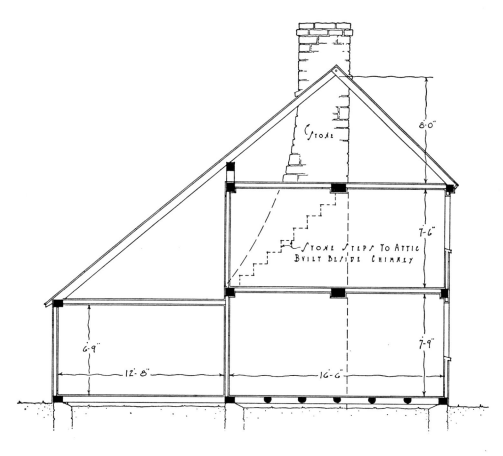

· CROSS SECTION ·

HAWLEY HOUSE-MONROE

FIGURE 207.

Chapter XVIII. Mouldings

IN the very earliest work, mouldings are conspicuously absent. During the early settlement of the first colonies, the main idea was to construct and not to decorate; utilitarianism reigned supreme. The colonist was face to face with too serious a proposition, time was too limited, and means were too scanty for the expenditure of any energies which were not directed toward the end of mere existence. We do not realize to-day how serious a problem confronted most of the first settlers.

It is entirely logical, accordingly, that the first mouldings should have been semi-utilitarian, like those at the joints of wainscot or the boards of batten doors. Where the broad boards used for wainscot were fastened together with the usual form of joint, consisting of a bevel and a quarter-round bead, such mouldings were constructive as well as ornamental. (Figure 174.) The joints of wainscot were formed with a "wainscot plough," all such material being worked out by hand. If the joints were merely halved together, as was often done with batten doors, the quirk mouldings which embellished the joints were purely decorative, for they served no constructive purpose. (Figure 155.) They and the chamfering of exposed beams may be regarded as the first deliberate attempt at ornamentation by means of mouldings. The chamfer, in its earliest and simplest form, consists merely of a bevelling of the corners of those portions of the oak framework which projected into the rooms. A typical example is the chamfering of the summer beams of the Dudley house in the town of Guilford (*circa* 1690), shown in Figure 76. The end of the bevel terminates in the common or lamb's-tongue form of chamfer stop. The two other examples shown in the same illustration have a more elaborate form of chamfer, actually moulded; and the stops show interesting variations of the simple and more rudimentary lamb's-tongue form. Elaborate and finely wrought chamfering, both exterior and interior, is a characteristic of the Guilford school. Moulded chamfers, corresponding in sectional contour to the *cyma erecta* and *cyma reversa* of Classical form, were cut into the timbers themselves. Such work is of the utmost interest, for it consists of frankly exposed structural forms to which a decorative treatment has been directly applied. Much of such work in Guilford is very early—as early as the last decade of the seventeenth century. Moulded chamfering, such as occurs on the exterior of the Hyland-Wildman house in Guilford (*circa* 1660), has not been noted elsewhere in Connecticut.

Ornamental mouldings (using the word in its modern sense) were probably not generally employed until late in the first half of the eighteenth century. Mouldings of this sort were made by hand from inch boards by means of special planes. The introduction of plastering and the resultant casings of exposed constructive members such as girts, posts, and summers, probably had much to do with such an innovation. The use of panelled wainscot across the fireplace wall brought about the treatment of the projecting chimney

General Cowles House—Farmington

Talmadge House—Litchfield

Old Tavern—Straitsville

Warner House—Chester

Plate XLVII.

girt as a cornice of Classical contour, especially where pilasters were employed in connection with the panelling. (Figure 168.) Cornices of this type usually consisted of a "crown moulding," or *cyma erecta* and fillet, a plain fascia, and two simple "bed mouldings" beneath it. A typical section is shown in Figure 149. Where pilasters are present, their capitals are formed by mitered projections of the bed mouldings—a satisfactory and ingenious arrangement. Moulding treatment of this sort, where employed in connection with the casing of the chimney girt, was generally extended along the summer beam and around the three remaining sides of the room.

Another early use of mouldings is to be seen in the treatment of fireplace openings. In their earliest forms, such mouldings were inclined to be somewhat crude and of bold projection, lacking in general *scale;* in other words they were out of proportion with the work which they were used to finish. (Figure 208.)

Indeed, mouldings of the earliest types were very generally lacking in grace and scale, and were of rather heavy and clumsy contour. Their principal characteristics, when they were used against a vertical surface, were boldness of projection and steepness of contour. These qualities were due, at first, to the literal adaptation of

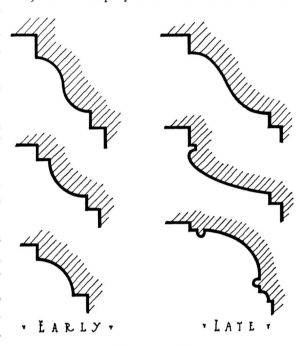

· EARLY ·   · LATE ·

FIGURE 208.

Classical forms primarily designed for an architecture of stone. Of some influence also was the fact that the English mouldings of the Jacobean period, as well as of that preceding it—which to some extent must have affected the early builders in America—were for the most part cut in stone, and were therefore very full and heavy in section.

Very soon after the introduction of mouldings there began an interesting development which may be regarded as a sort of evolution or process of refinement. Continuing through various periods, it reached its culmination only during the time which corresponds to the Adam era in England. In translating the proportions of Classical models into a new material, the American craftsman, working in wood, was not hampered by the limitations which bound him to certain observances in using stone. Thin edges could be formed of wood without danger of breakage or chipping, and flatter projections than those of the conventional forty-five degree angle were made possible without serious loss of strength.

Besides this increasing fineness of scale and detail, two other considerations came to be expressed: first, the lightness and flexibility of the new material; and, secondly, the fact that work executed in it existed primarily for the sake of its appearance, and not as an embodiment of rules of construction. The Classic cornice, for instance, when executed in stone, is *built up* of successive imposed courses, each member being designed actually to carry that above it. Such construction is logical; there is a definite reason for every member. In the cornice built up of wooden mouldings, this principle became lost. The bed mouldings, for example, in a Classical cornice, are sturdy and of short projection; their office is to support the members above them. In the wooden cornice, especially in late examples, the bed mouldings became a flattened cove of great projection, the purpose of which was primarily to soften the line of an internal angle.

It may appear at first glance that such construction in wood was not so true architecturally as the model upon which it was based; but the point is not well taken. The inherent nature of the new material made the building up of superimposed members unnecessary; and a frank and open expression of this fact cannot be called false.

In appraising the development of wooden mouldings, the influence of Wren's school must be given due weight. Through constant intercourse with England, the spirit of Georgian work there was bound to be felt in, and, to a considerable extent, infused into, American work. Furniture was constantly being brought from England, and the influence of the cabinetmakers there was also a factor in the process of refinement. Moreover various books, published in England on the subject of architecture, or, more properly, building—books such as those of Asher Benjamin—helped to shape the work being done in America.

In endeavoring to assign a definite period to certain mouldings, considerable difficulty is met with; for the same forms and quality of workmanship were not extant everywhere in Connecticut during a given time. Work which is primitive in conception or crude in execution is not necessarily of an early period; for, as in other matters, greater advancement and finer finish were the products of the more thickly populated regions, the towns. In poorer or more remote locations, far from the main highways which formed the main arteries of intercourse, less expert work may naturally be expected. Some regions were also much more conservative than others, more tardy in adopting innovations. In a general way, however, certain sections or contours are peculiar to the mouldings used during a given period. It is interesting to trace, as may sometimes be done, the development of a moulding of given section from its earliest appearance through successive changes to an ultimate or final form. Three mouldings of common form are shown in Figure 208. It will be seen that in their early forms they are literal adaptations from Classical examples cut in stone. In their later forms, the early steepness of the projection has given way to considerably flattened shapes which are finer in scale and far more graceful in outline than the originals from which they developed.

As before stated, mouldings were made entirely by hand with a set of specially designed planes. Often two or even three planes were necessary to produce a moulding of given section. Inasmuch as every builder had his own set of planes, the individual builder often employed mouldings or combinations of mouldings which remained peculiar to his work and strongly flavored by his taste. The handicraft of a certain man may very often be

Hinges, latch handles, bolts, and various other articles of hardware used in the early Connecticut house were, for the most part, forged from wrought iron. Occasionally latch handles of brass are to be found (Figure 211), but they are rare by comparison with those of iron. Door knockers, though, were generally of brass; and it is probable that a good many of them were of English manufacture.

The remarkably good state of preservation in which various articles exist to-day, after perhaps a century and a half of unprotected exposure to the elements, indicates without question the purity of the iron from which they were forged. Iron which contains but few impurities does not rust or oxidize rapidly; instead, it gradually becomes covered with a thin protecting coat of patina.

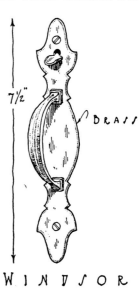

FIGURE 211.

The early Court Records of New Haven contain numerous allusions to the manufacture of iron from the ore. Under the date of March 16, 1654/55 we read: "Mr. Goodyeare desired, if they knew of any Ironstone aboute this Towne, they would make it knowne, that now Mr. Winthrop* is here he may be gotten to judg of it, and if it prove right, and that an Iron mill might be set up here it would be a great advantag to the Towne." The minutes of a "General Court held for New Haven Y^e 29th of Novemr 1655" contain the following: "The Governor informed ye Towne that this meeting was called to consider something further aboute the Iron workes. Sundrie who ingaged to work last Court have not yet performed, though others have, and it was now concluded that those that are behinde should be called upon to performe what they promised. It was also now desired that men will declare, who will ingage in the worke, and what estate they will put in; but few speaking to it, it was desired that those who are willing would meete at the Governors this afternoon at two a clocke, to declare themselves therein, and it was now propounded whether the Towne will give up their rights in Ye place, and what accomodation is necessary for the best conveniency of the said iron worke, & in this case all the Towne voted to give a full libertie for Ye Iron-workes to goe on & also for wood, water, Iron-ston, oare, shells for lime, or whatever else is necessary for that worke, upon Ye Townes land, or that side of Ye great river, called the East river; provided that no mans proprietie laid out or to be laid out be intrenched upon, nor no planter prohibitted from cutting wood or other conveniency upon the said common in an orderly way, and that Branford doe make the like grant, according to the proportion they have in the worke, that further questions aboute this thing may be prevented." The iron works are next mentioned in the record of May 19, 1656, as follows: "Upon a motion made by Mr. Goodyeare and John Coop^r on behalfe of the Collier that comes to burn coale for the Iron-worke, he have twelve ac^rs of land granted to him as his owne, if the Iron-worke goe on, and he stay three yeares in the worke; provided that all minneralls ther be

* John the younger, of New London.

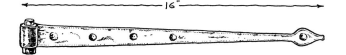

FIGURE 212.

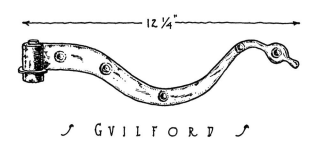

ſ GVILFORD ſ

FIGURE 213.

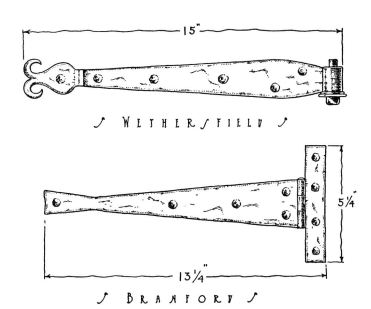

ſ WETHERſFIELD ſ

ſ BRANFORD ſ

FIGURE 214.

reserved, and that he attend all Yᵉ orders of the Towne, for Yᵉ present, and in disposing of the said land hereafter, if it shall so fall out. The place propounded for to have it in, is upon the beavor meddow, conteyning a hundred or two hundred acʳˢ, aboute two miles from Yᵉ Iron worke; against wᶜʰ grant or place none objected so as to hinder Yᵉ same." A final

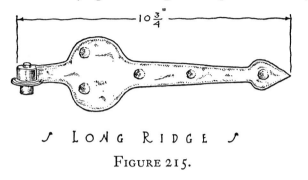

♪ LONG RIDGE ♪

FIGURE 215.

allusion to this undertaking is made in the record of February 19, 1685, in which a furnace and a "forge or two" are mentioned.

The early manufacture of iron in Connecticut is also noted by Lambert, who states that a mill was established in 1655 in the colony of New Haven by John Winthrop, Jr., and Stephen Goodyear. It was situated at the southern end of Lake Saltonstall, and was in operation up to 1679-1680, at which time it was abandoned. The work of producing iron at the "Bloomery" there ceased very abruptly; for what reason, it is not known. The ore, a sesquioxide of iron, was brought from North Haven, where existed a deposit covering a considerable area. Dodd of East Haven states in his *Register:* "Why this business was relinquished cannot be satisfactorily ascertained. The furnace was supplied with bog-ore from North Haven. It was chiefly carted, but sometimes brought

from Bogmine Wharf by water round to the Point below the furnace and from that circumstance the Point to this day is called 'Bogmine.' "

Iron was "wrought at the forges" of old Newgate Prison in East Granby, and large quantities of nails were manufactured there by the prisoners. It is probable that nails were forged at New Haven at a very early date from iron

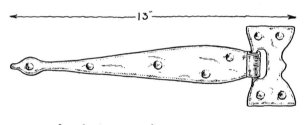

♪ NORTH LYME ♪

FIGURE 216.

brought from England, for the Court Records of 1644 make mention of "John Thompson, nayler," and those of 1648 order that "Whosoever shall sell nailes in this town shall sell six score to yᵉ hundred."

According to tradition, a considerable amount of various sorts of hardware was turned out by individual craftsmen who worked at their own forges in different localities. This usage may largely account for the broad diversity of forms in which certain articles appear. Owing to their general lack of similarity, it is somewhat difficult to make coherent groups of the types of latches, hinges, and other products, and the classification can be accomplished only in a broad way.

The earliest types of door hinges are undoubtedly those of strap form, such as are shown in Figure 212. Hinges of this variety are usually very long: specimens measuring two feet or more in length are not uncommon. The butt end of each hinge was formed into an eye, which was hung upon a shouldered iron peg driven into the door jamb. Strap hinges were used more than any other variety for hanging exterior doors, and their use there persisted until a fairly late date. The "snake" hinge (Figure 213) is a pleasing variation which does not commonly occur in Connecticut. It is plainly an attempt at decorative

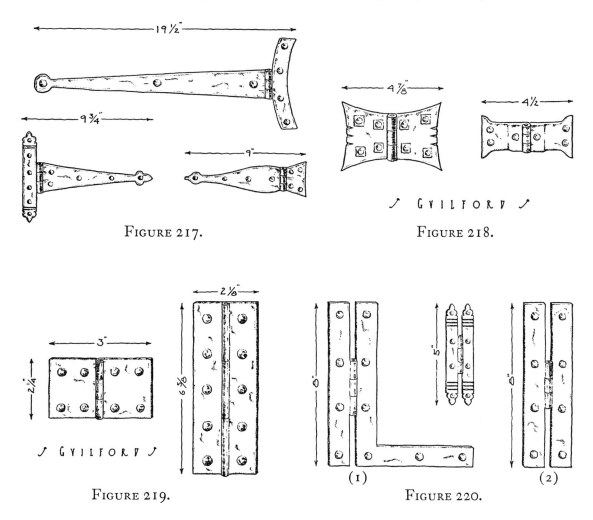

FIGURE 217.

FIGURE 218.

FIGURE 219.

FIGURE 220.

form, and its undulant outline is very pleasing. This specimen was in use on an inside door, as were the two hinges shown in Figure 214. The upper example shown in this illustration is unusual because of its bifurcated termination; that beneath it is noteworthy because it shows a transitional form which developed from the strap hinge. A somewhat similar, though possibly earlier, specimen is shown in Figure 216. A plate of more or less ornamental form has replaced the peg of the earlier type. This hinge is a rare specimen; the writer has seen its like but twice in Connecticut. Three other examples of "half-strap" form are shown in Figure 217. The two lower hinges in the illustration were taken from cupboard

Deming House—Farmington

Bronze Knocker—Chester

"Historical House"—South Norwalk

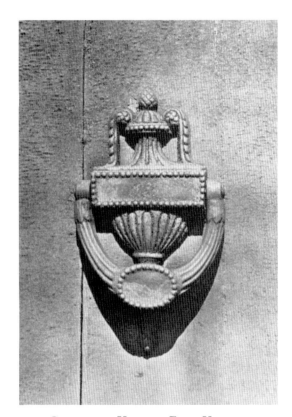

Champion House—East Haddam

Plate XLVIII.

doors; that above them is a regular door hinge. Eventually this strap form disappeared, and a hinge which more resembled the modern "butt" took its place.

The "butterfly" hinge, shown on the left in Figure 218, is a very old form of English origin. It occurs on chests of English workmanship which date back to the sixteenth century. The hinge shown to the right of it is a later variation. Both were serving on cupboard doors. The three cuts or notches on either outside margin of the butterfly hinge illustrated

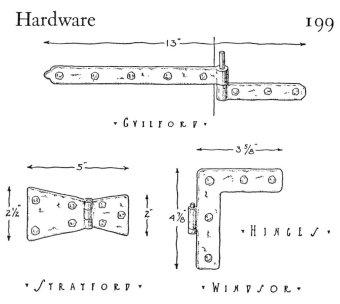

FIGURE 221.

are common characteristics; so are the leather washers inserted under the heads of the nails by which it is secured. Red morocco leather was generally used for this purpose; its brilliant color, where it has not been obscured by successive coats of paint, makes it of considerable decorative value. Sometimes leather was also used in this same manner in fastening hinges of earlier type, such as those of strap form. Butterfly hinges were principally used in hanging cupboard doors, though larger forms were sometimes used for regular inside doors as well. The transition is easy from hinges of the butterfly type to specimens which more resemble the modern article, such as those shown in Figure 219. The somewhat fanciful shape and graceful outline have given way to a simple, purely utilitarian form.

Two familiar forms of hinge, both very commonly used, are shown in Figure 220. They are known as (1) the H-and-L and (2) the H hinge. Not so early as the strap hinge, they were widely used until a very late date; sometimes they occur in work of 1800 or even later. H and H-and-L hinges were used more commonly than any other variety for hanging interior doors; in fact, they appear to have been the conventional forms for this purpose. Their average measurement is about eight or nine inches, though here and there specimens are found of much greater size. Those on the front door of the Captain Ambrose Whittlesey house in Saybrook (1799) are thirteen inches wide and the same in height. H-and-L

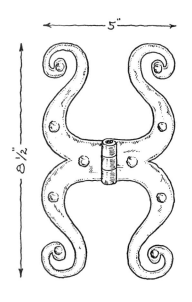

FIGURE 222.

hinges are rarely used in this manner for hanging exterior doors: strap hinges were the favorite sort for that purpose. A more decorative form of the H hinge is also shown in Figure 220. Hinges of this sort, of three lobed termination and cross scored, were generally used for inside shutters and cupboard doors.

The hinge shown in Figure 222 is an extremely rare and unusually elaborate form. When discovered, it was serving as a barn door hinge; but it is not probable that it was originally wrought for such a purpose. An equally rare specimen is that illustrated in Figure 223. Its decorative form reaches far back into antiquity, the "cock's head" terminations which it displays being a traditional heritage from Roman times. In the house from which this hinge was taken, similar specimens were serving on wall and corner cupboard doors.

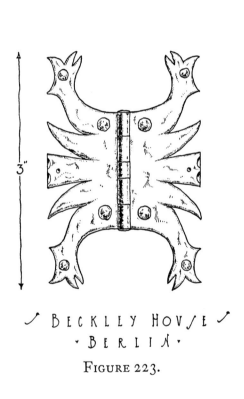

√ BECKLEY HOUSE √
· BERLIN ·

FIGURE 223.

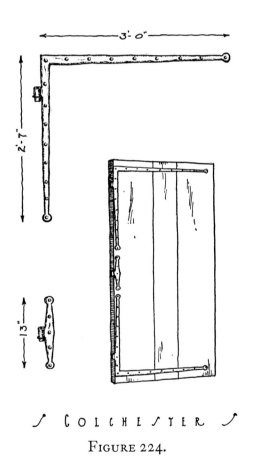

√ COLCHESTER √

FIGURE 224.

The set of exterior door hinges from the Deming house in Colchester (1771), illustrated in Figure 224, are splendid specimens. They have not only an ornamental value, but a structural one as well, for their great size and peculiar shape make the door much more rigid and add to its strength.

A study of latches and, more particularly, of their handles, unearths many striking and curious specimens. The broad diversity of forms to be encountered on every hand, together with the general lack of similarity in design except in the simplest examples, speaks eloquently of the skilled artistry of the men who forged them.

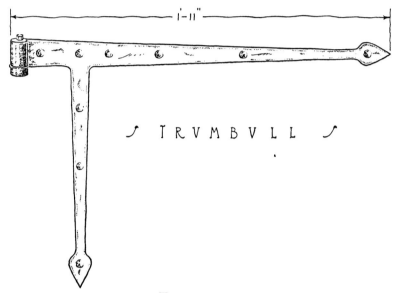

FIGURE 225.

A great proportion of such latch handles, especially those of an early period, designed for use on outside doors, were of comparatively large size. Those shown in Figures 226 and 227 are early forms; both are bold and vigorous in design. Notches, or V-shaped incisions in the handle, such as the specimen shows in Figure 228, are a common feature. In some instances an attempt at ornamentation was made by scoring the handles with horizontal cuts from a chisel or other edged tool. The iron latch shown in Figure 229, from an outside door of the Chaffee house in Windsor, bears the date of building of the house (1776), pricked into the handle. What is perhaps the most typical form of iron latch handle to be found in Connecticut is that illustrated in Figure 230. The use of square bits of red Morocco leather under the nail heads is characteristic.

The latch handle shown in Figure 231, though of common form, is extraordinary in size; and for this reason it is a decorative feature of much interest and value. Although

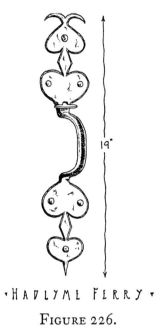

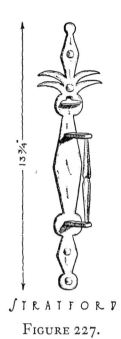

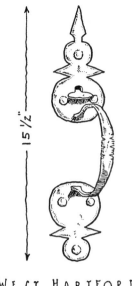

·HADLYME FERRY·

FIGURE 226.

STRATFORD

FIGURE 227.

WEST HARTFORD

FIGURE 228.

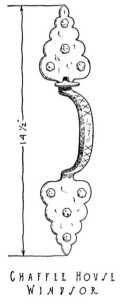

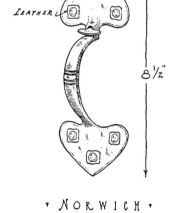

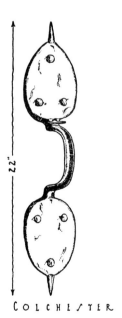

CHAFFEE HOUSE
WINDSOR

FIGURE 229.

·NORWICH·

FIGURE 230.

COLCHESTER

FIGURE 231.

not strictly within the confines of domestic architecture, a wrought-iron latch handle from the church door at Middle Haddam, one of unusual size and exceedingly handsome form, is illustrated in Figure 232.

Specimens such as those shown in Figure 233, though they represent a very common type, belong to a much later period. They are of much smaller size than those earlier in use; and being, apparently, "shop made," they are of considerably less interest than the foregoing examples, which were all hand-wrought. The little fillet of pewter applied to the handle is a characteristic feature of latches of this type. The use of small-headed nails in place of the hand-forged variety with large flat heads detracts considerably from the general interest and decorative value of these latches of later type.

It is quite probable that, during the earliest period of the colony, wooden latches, such as the one shown in Figure 235, were in common use, especially on doors in the less important parts of the house —e.g., those of the rear rooms and those on the second floor. The latch from which the illustration was made was on a door opening from the kitchen chamber of the Caleb Dudley house in Guilford, built about 1690, and is doubtlessly as old as the house itself. A somewhat similar latch of wood secures a door of one of the rear rooms on the second floor of the Graves house in Madison (1675). Latches of this sort possess that oft-quoted feature, the latch-string.

During the latter part of the eighteenth century the wrought-iron latches gave way to the iron lock of familiar form. This was applied to the surface of the door, and operated by a small egg-shaped knob of brass. Such locks were not often mortised into the doors, as is customary to-day. This type of inside door fastening is frequently met with as a part of work built after 1800.

In addition to the arrangement of a horizontal wooden bar across the inner side of an exterior door, various forms of wrought-iron bolts were common means of outside door fastening. Two typical specimens are shown in Figure 237. Locks did not come into general use until after Revolutionary times. Early examples are very often fitted with clumsy wooden casings, such as that illustrated in Figure 238. The working parts, of course, are of metal.

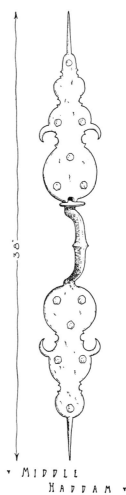

MIDDLE
HADDAM
FIGURE 232.

Several specimens of hand-forged nails are shown in Figure 239. Their use covers a wide period, from very early until—in some parts of Connecticut—after 1800. Wrought-iron nails were used in every part of the house construction except in fastening together the oak framework, for which purpose, of course, oaken pegs were used. The smallest nail shown in the illustration is of the sort used in finishing interior woodwork, especially mouldings. Its peculiar shape was such that it could be driven into woodwork so that its head did not remain exposed. It was accordingly the "finishing-nail" of early days.

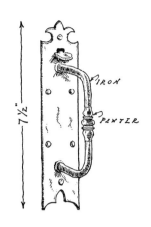

IRON

PEWTER

SHELTON

FIGURE 233.

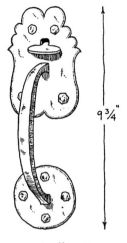

9¾"

PITKIN HOVSE
EAST HARTFORD

FIGURE 234.

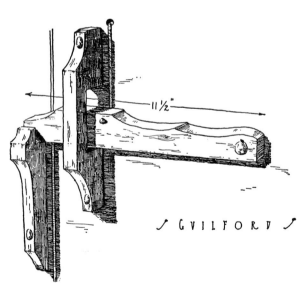

11½"

GVILFORD

FIGURE 235.

11¾"

BECKLEY HOVSE
BERLIN

FIGURE 236.

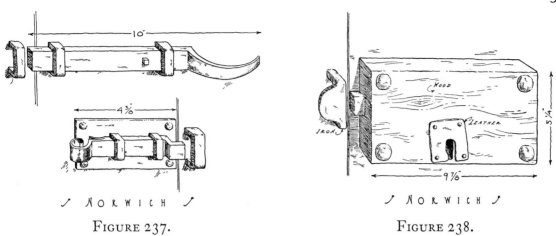

FIGURE 237. FIGURE 238.

Wrought-iron nails were succeeded in use by machine-made "cut nails," probably because of their comparative cheapness, which was in turn due to greater ease of production. Not only were they inferior in strength and lasting qualities to the hand-forged variety, but they lacked the large flattened heads of the earlier sort. A decorative feature of considerable value was accordingly lost with the passing of the hand-wrought nail. A house

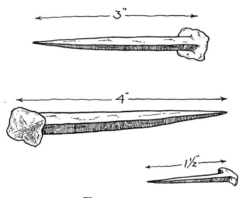

FIGURE 239.

covered with clapboards, laid in courses of graduated exposure and secured by wrought nails with irregularly shaped heads of one-half- or three-fourths-inch diameter, occurring at regular intervals, possesses a distinction which is entirely lacking where no nail heads appear.

The great majority of the various forms of knockers which adorn the front entrance doors of so many old houses do not date back so far as the houses themselves. As most of them exhibit strong Adam influence, they are necessarily of comparatively late workmanship. Knockers were not employed on the doors of the earliest houses; knuckles served instead. The wrought-iron knocker shown in Figure 240, from the front door of the older

Silliman house near Fairfield (*circa* 1730), is undoubtedly of very early workmanship: possibly it is of English make. The knocker illustrated in Plate XLVIII from the Warner house near Chester (1793) is an unusually fine specimen. It is made of cast bronze, and beautifully finished. A cast-iron knocker from the so-called Historical House in Norwalk (*circa* 1750) is also shown in Plate XLVIII. Most door knockers, however, were of cast brass, polished and buffed to a high finish. It is probable that they were largely produced in England and imported to this country. Cast-iron specimens such as that shown in Plate

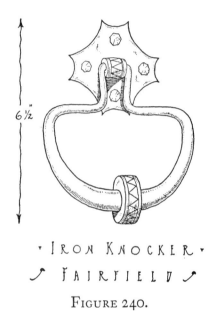

· IRON KNOCKER ·

ﬀ FAIRFIELD ﬀ

FIGURE 240.

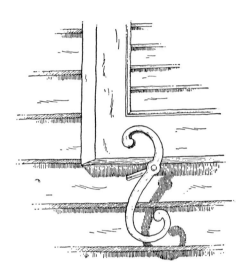

FIGURE 241.

XLVIII do not occur so commonly as brass, for, unless plated with some non-rusting metal or else painted, they soon became disfigured with rust. One of the chief attractions of the brass knocker is the resplendent polish which may be produced by diligent rubbing. The iron knocker which is illustrated was originally plated with "water gilt," traces of which still remain. It is on the side or garden door of the Champion house in East Haddam (1794).

Blind catches of familiar form, constructed of wrought iron, must also be included in a discussion of hardware. A typical specimen is illustrated in Figure 241. Since the blind was a late feature, these fastenings were also of late date.

Wrought-iron foot scrapers occur commonly and in many forms. Often strikingly handsome in design, they display a great deal of style and elegance as well as of skilled and careful workmanship. They, too, belong to a late period.

The discussion of this topic cannot be closed without at least a brief mention of the iron cranes which still hang in so many fireplaces. They are generally to be found—or so, at least, are the eyes which supported them, driven into the masonry—in the fireplaces of the hall and kitchen (for these were the rooms in which the cooking was done). Some of these old cranes still retain their full complement of pot hooks and trammel bars—the latter being adjustable arrangements for hanging kettles at any desired height above the fire. Now and then a fireplace is found which has only a straight iron bar extending across it, built into the masonry on either side. This arrangement is not so common as the crane; but it is perhaps even more antique.

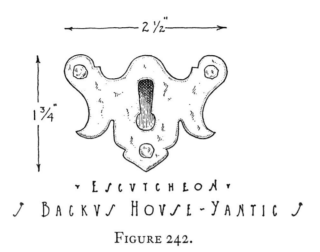

FIGURE 242.

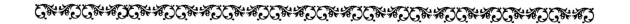

Index